The House of Hapsburg

The Spanish Hapsburgs

The Hapsburgs in
Central Europe

Empires

Their Rise and Fall

The House of Hapsburg

The Spanish Hapsburgs

The Hapsburgs in Central Europe

Joyce Milton
The Spanish Hapsburgs

Caroline Davidson
The Hapsburgs in Central Europe

Preface by Barbara Jelavich
Professor of History
Indiana University

Boston Publishing Company, Inc.
Boston, Massachusetts

Empires: Their Rise and Fall is published in the United States by Boston Publishing Company, Inc., and distributed by Field Publications.

Authors: Joyce Milton, Caroline Davidson
Picture Researcher, Janet Adams
Assistant Picture Researcher, Lynn Bowdery
Historical Consultant, Professor James Miller
Project Consultant, Valerie Hopkins
Design Implementation, Designworks

Boston Publishing Company, Inc.

President, Robert J. George
Editor-In-Chief, Robert Manning
Managing Editor, Paul Dreyfus
Marketing Director, Jeanne Gibson

Field Publications

President, Bruce H. Seide
Publisher, Marilyn Black
Marketing Director, Kathleen E. Long

Rizzoli Editore

Authors of the Italian Edition
    Introduction: Professor Ovidio Dallera
    The Spanish Hapsburgs: Professor Gherardo Bozzetti
    The Hapsburgs in Central Europe: Dr. Flavio Conti
    Maps: Gian Franco Leonardi
Idea and Realization, Harry C. Lindinger
Graphic Design, Gerry Valsecchi
General Editorial Supervisor, Ovidio Dallera

© 1987 by Rizzoli Editore
Printed in the United States.

Library of Congress Catalog Card Number: 79-2521
ISBN: 0-15-004031-8

Contents

Preface

An account of the fortunes of the House of Hapsburg provides a unique story of a noble family whose influence extended over seven centuries and three continents. Holding possessions inhabited by peoples of differing nationality, historical tradition, and social composition, Hapsburg monarchs attempted to establish political institutions that would unite their subjects under a supranational authority. As a result of the many years of Hapsburg rule, a deep imprint was left on the cultural, political, and social life of much of Europe and the Americas.

The Hapsburgs take their name from their ancestral castle of Habichtsburg, in present-day Switzerland. ("Habichtsburg" was in time contracted to "Habsburg," which has been Anglicized as "Hapsburg.") From the tenth century onward, the family gradually amassed lands through inheritance, marriage, and conquest. At its height under Charles V in the sixteenth century, the Hapsburg Empire included lands in central Europe, Italy, and the Low Countries, as well as Spain and its colonies in the Americas. The impracticality of governing these scattered territories led to the administrative division of the empire in 1522, with Charles V entrusting the central European inheritance to his younger brother, Ferdinand. In 1556, Charles' son, Philip II, succeeded to the throne of Spain. Thereafter one family did indeed reign in two empires.

The period of Hapsburg rule in Spain marks the golden age of Spanish civilization and the height of Spanish political power. This was the epoch that produced the great paintings of El Greco, Murillo, and Velázquez and the celebrated literary works of Cervantes and Calderón de la Barca. In the sixteenth century, Spaniards organized an extensive colonial empire, settling America from Florida to California and south through Central and South America.

With the extinction of the Hapsburg male line in 1700 and the passing of the Spanish throne to the French Bourbon dynasty, Hapsburg rule was confined to central Europe. There the family held, in addition to its hereditary provinces in Austria, the possessions associated with the Bohemian and Hungarian Crowns and various other lands in Italy and the Low Countries. Still other regions, inhabited by Slavs, Italians, and Romanians, were acquired later. The major problem facing the Hapsburg monarchs was to find a basis of government for a state that contained eleven principal nationalities, all with different traditions and customs.

In their efforts to organize and consolidate their territories, the Hapsburg emperors met opposition from both foreign and domestic foes. French kings, Ottoman sultans, and German princes repeatedly challenged Hapsburg power. Within the state the local nobility fiercely fought any attempts at centralization. An ultimately fatal influence was exerted by the rising nationalism of nineteenth-century Europe. After the unification of Germany and Italy and the formation of the Balkan national states, the desire for political autonomy and the free expression of cultural individuality became increasingly strong among the various nationalities of the Hapsburg realm. Hapsburg statesmen tried but failed to find a common base or a popular principle to offset the disintegrating force of this nationalism.

Hapsburg rulers dealt with the chief issues of internal and external politics on a direct and daily basis. With only infrequent exceptions, the monarchs were dedicated and able men. Faithful members of the Catholic Church, they felt responsible to God for the welfare of their lands. Three rulers of the eighteenth, nineteenth, and twentieth centuries—Maria Theresa, Joseph II, and Francis Joseph—ranked among the foremost sovereigns of Europe. All attempted to establish standards of efficiency and justice and to balance the conflicting interests of their people.

Despite the growing political controversies, the Hapsburg monarchy and the Hapsburg capital at Vienna remained the center of a cosmopolitan cultural life. Music proved to be the major achievement, with one generation of composers alone including Haydn, Mozart, Beethoven, and Schubert. Popular music was enriched by the waltzes of the Strauss family and the operettas of Lehár. In the last decades of the monarchy's existence, Vienna was the home of the painters Klimt and Kokoschka, the composers Mahler and Schönberg, and the psychologist Freud—each a pioneer in his field.

The Hapsburgs, whose rule came to an end in Spain in 1700 and in central Europe in 1918, held power in both regions during a period of cultural and political ascendancy. By helping to produce an environment favorable to artistic accomplishment, they contributed greatly to the cultural legacy of modern Europe.

BARBARA JELAVICH
Professor of History
Indiana University

The Spanish Hapsburgs

In 1477, Frederick of Hapsburg, duke of Austria and Holy Roman emperor, borrowed traveling money from a prominent banking family and set out for Trier, in what is now West Germany. His mission—to negotiate a marriage contract between his son Maximilian and Mary of Burgundy, the daughter of Charles the Bold and Margaret of York. Despite his august titles, Frederick commanded little power and less wealth. His ancestral lands had been overrun by the army of King Matthias Corvinus of Hungary, and the silver mines of the Tyrolean region, his major financial asset, were heavily mortgaged. Frederick

Preceding page, the Escorial, the historic monastery and royal residence northwest of Madrid built by King Philip II (1527–1598).

Separated from the mainland mass of Europe by the natural barrier of the Pyrenees, Spain consists of a high central plateau ringed by granite massifs, including the Sierra Morena in the southwest (above). Right, the steep gorges of the Segre River region in northeastern Spain.

The topography of the Iberian Peninsula led to the rise and maintenance of strong regional traditions. The Sierra Nevada (right) transects Granada, a province long a bastion of Spain's Morisco and Jewish minorities.

Granada's climate resembles that of nearby North Africa. Facing page, below left, dwellings in Granada, set into the hillsides to provide a refuge from the summer heat.

brought to Trier little but hope and an unshakable faith in the destiny of the House of Hapsburg.

Charles the Bold, the man Frederick had come to bargain with, was dealing from a position of strength. As ruler of the prosperous duchy of Burgundy, which at that time controlled Flanders, he presided over the most splendid court in Europe, a fairy-tale society that passed its days and nights in a seemingly endless round of jousting, hunting, and pageantry. Patrons of music, collectors of tapestries and illuminated manuscripts, and employers of such celebrated painters as Rogier van der Weyden and the van Eycks, the Burgundian nobility saw both the mature flowering of the chivalric ideal and the first stirrings of Renaissance consciousness.

The one thing that Charles the Bold lacked—the title of king—was a dignity that Frederick, as Holy Roman emperor, was able to arrange. If the meeting at Trier had gone as planned, Burgundy might have become a kingdom, equal in status to its great rival, France. Negotiations, however, broke down, and Charles, rushing off to contend with the army of Louis XI of France, was killed in battle that same year.

Nevertheless, the wedding of Mary and Maximilian was celebrated in 1477, largely because everyone from the love-struck bride and her mother to the townspeople of Burgundy preferred the Austrian bridegroom to his likely alternative, the dauphin of France. For the penniless Frederick, the match was a triumph. Legend has it that his nemesis, Matthias Corvinus, was sufficiently impressed to pen this playful couplet:

The strong make war; thou, happy Austria, marry.
What Mars gives to others, Venus grants to thee.

Thus raised by Venus into the lap of Burgundian luxury, the nineteen-year-old Maximilian displayed a gift that few of his descendants would share: the ability to enjoy himself. Gregarious and witty, Maximilian plunged into the round of court festivities. "I have danced a good deal, and tilted lances and enjoyed carnival," he once wrote. "I have paid court to the ladies and earned great thanks; for the most part I have laughed heartily."

Maximilian, though, experienced his share of troubles as well. His beloved wife, Mary, died in a hunting accident when she was only twenty-four; Vienna, his father's capital, was captured by Matthias Corvinus in 1485; and Maximilian himself, not long after being named King of the Romans—a title bestowed

on the heir of the Holy Roman emperor—endured the humiliation of being held prisoner for four months by rebellious subjects who bristled at the prospect of paying for their ruler's foreign excursions. When Maximilian, undaunted, decided that a second marriage would be the best solution to his chronic cash shortage, he scandalized Europe by wedding Bianca Sforza, daughter of the parvenu duke of Milan.

Toward the end of his life, the increasingly eccentric Maximilian even toyed with the idea of becoming pope. In a playful letter to his daughter, he outlined his scheme for bribing the College of Cardinals and eventually buying his way to sainthood. "You will then have to worship me when I am dead, which will be delightful," he wrote. To the relief of everyone, Maximilian's offer to pawn the crown jewels in exchange for the papal office came to naught.

Mary of Burgundy, Maximilian's first wife, bore two children, Margaret and Philip. Philip became duke of Burgundy upon his mother's death, but the less fortunate Margaret was brought up in virtual captivity as the intended bride of the dauphin of France. When circumstances forced the dauphin to seek a wife elsewhere, Maximilian wasted no time in marrying Margaret to the son of Ferdinand and Isabella of Spain—and Philip to their daughter.

Politically, the double marriage was a master stroke; biologically, it was a disaster. A tendency toward insanity ran in Isabella's family: Her father, mother, and half brother had all been mad. No one recognized the implications of this at the time, and considerations of health would not have been allowed to interfere with what was basically an affair of state in any case. But the young couples had not been married long before certain abnormalities became manifest.

The first signs of trouble came from Prince Juan, the only son of Ferdinand and Isabella and the heir to the combined thrones of Castile and Aragon. From the day of his marriage to Margaret, Juan threw

Top left, a valley between the cities of Valencia and Alicante in Spain. The province of Valencia, on Spain's Mediterranean coast, is celebrated for its mild climate and prosperous orange groves. Center left, the fertile countryside of Granada. Bottom left, a landscape near Segovia, a city in central Spain. Above right, the Costa del Sol near Gibraltar. Near right, the Atlantic coast of Spain between Gibraltar and Cádiz. Far right, the Tagus River as it widens into a long lake in southern Castile.

himself into his marital duties with such passion that his mother feared for his health. Her apprehensions proved justified: Eighteen months later, Juan was dead.

Juana, newly married to Philip, Margaret's brother, also proved to be inordinately interested in lovemaking. In her case, sensuality took the form of an almost religious devotion to her husband's body. Although recognizably insane, Juana had far more stamina than her unhappy brother. She bore her husband six children and after her mother's death traveled with Philip to Castile, where in 1506 they were named corulers.

The young couple had reigned for only six months before Philip, seemingly so strong and healthy, suddenly died. The shock of widowhood destroyed the last remnants of Juana's sanity. The distraught queen refused to allow her husband's body to be buried, insisting that the coffin be brought with her wherever she went in the hope that Philip could be resurrected to share her bed once again. After three years, Ferdinand returned to Castile to assume the regency for his daughter, and Juana, who became known as *la Loca* ("the Mad"), was sent to a convent, where she lived for over forty years, until her death in 1555.

In Burgundy, meanwhile, Juana's eldest son,

Above, the eleventh-century alcazar of Segovia, a fortress built when Segovia was the capital of Moorish Spain. It later became a favorite residence of the Christian kings of Castile. Near right, the alcazar's Hall of the Ambassadors. The main façade of the alcazar of Seville (below far right) was completed by King Pedro I of Portugal in the fourteenth century. Left, the Court of Myrtles in the Alhambra, the palace and fortress of the Moorish rulers of Granada. The Alcazaba of Málaga (above far right) is a restored Moorish fortress of the ninth century.

Charles of Ghent, was growing up in the household of his paternal aunt Margaret. After the death of his father, six-year-old Charles had come into the Burgundian inheritance, which comprised the Franche-Comté (a region in the east-central part of present-day France), Luxembourg, and the area that is today Holland and Belgium. Through his father and grandfather he also stood to receive the archduchy of Austria and the original Hapsburg domains on the upper Rhine.

It had never been expected that the same individual who ruled these territories would also become king of Spain, but this disconcerting prospect soon loomed as a virtual certainty. The premature deaths of Prince Juan, Juan's elder sister, and this sister's young son had made Juana and Philip heirs to Castile; with Philip dead and Juana disabled, it became likely that Charles would take over the government of Castile as soon as he became of age. In addition, Charles was heir to his grandfather Ferdinand's kingdom of Aragon, which encompassed the provinces of Aragon, Catalonia, and Valencia, as well as the kingdoms of Navarre, Naples, and Sicily.

This development was not at all pleasing to the wily and ambitious Ferdinand, who had been bitterly stung by his exclusion from the will of his wife, Isa-

bella. Remarried to the beautiful Germaine de Foix, Ferdinand hoped desperately for a son who would provide some excuse to contest the claims of the Burgundian relatives he had come to detest. (Gossip had it that the old king dosed himself with potency restorers to the extent that his health was undermined.) The couple's only child did not survive, however, and when Ferdinand died in 1516 his possessions passed to the sixteen-year-old Charles.

The young man who became King Charles I of Spain seemed very poorly equipped for the role fate had cast him in. His chief interests in life were horseback riding and eating, and he was neither a connoisseur of the arts like so many of his countrymen nor a bon vivant in the style of his grandfather Maximilian. His physical appearance was marred by the notorious Hapsburg jaw. This family trait, which was present in a milder form in Maximilian and perhaps also in Maximilian's first wife, Mary of Burgundy, is evidence of a condition known as acrocephaly; its cause, an inherited endocrine dysfunction, is also associated with epilepsy and a tendency toward nervous disorders. The extreme psychological manifestations of the condition had passed Charles by, but the overdeveloped jaw made it impossible for him to chew his food or even to close his mouth. A Spanish subject is

said to have once taunted Charles by saying: "Your Majesty, close your mouth, for the flies in this country are very insolent."

When Charles traveled to Spain in 1517, his unfortunate appearance was just one factor working against him. The Castilians had hated Charles' father when he ruled them briefly as Philip I, and they were equally unenthusiastic about his son, who spoke not a word of the Castilian language and brought with himself a flood of Burgundian office seekers, sycophants, and hangers-on.

Dissatisfaction with Charles was heightened by the availability of a more appealing candidate for the throne. Ferdinand, Charles' younger brother by three years, was Spanish-educated and universally well

Above, the deed of surrender signed in 1493 by Boabdil, the last Moorish king of Granada. Below, the king handing over the keys to the city.

Above, the walled city of Ávila. A well-preserved remnant of medieval Spain, Ávila is a typically Castilian city. Situated fifty-four miles west of Madrid on the Adaja River, it is surrounded by the soaring Sierra de Gredos to the south and the Sierra de Guadarrama to the east. Presumed to be of Phoenician origin, Ávila was part of the Roman Lusitania before falling to the Moors of North Africa in 714. The dark granite walls of the city were built in the eleventh century by Raymond of Burgundy. Including 88 cubos (cylindrical towers) and nine gates, the walls encompassed the whole of ancient Ávila. The expulsion of the Moriscos in 1607–1610 dealt the city's commerce and industry a severe blow, from which they never fully recovered.

Columbus and Queen Isabella

The year 1492, which saw the termination of Moorish rule in Granada, the expulsion of the Jews from Spain, and the publication of the first Castilian grammar, also witnessed the first of Christopher Columbus' voyages to the New World. The decision of Queen Isabella of Spain to sponsor Columbus seems to have been doubly motivated. First, Isabella wanted a share in the lucrative spice trade that the Portuguese were at the time conducting with the Indies; second, she hoped that the discovery of a new route to the East would undermine the power of the Ottoman Turks. She could not have foreseen that Columbus' journey would lay the foundations for a Castilian empire in the New World—an empire that would increase the territory under Castilian sway twofold and provide much-needed gold for the strained national economy.

The Castilian heirs of the crusaders who had reclaimed southern Spain from the Moors proved to be less interested in trade with the peoples of the New World than in booty and settlement. These latter privileges were reserved in Isabella's will for Castilians—to the ultimate detriment of Spanish unity.

Above left, a portrait of Columbus attributed to the fifteenth-century Florentine artist Domenico Ghirlandajo. Immediately above, Columbus' first landfall in the New World: San Salvador Island in the Bahamas.

Above, the earliest known chart of the New World. This map is by Juan de la Cosa, who took part in Columbus' first two voyages to America. Left, a compass card, a typical piece of equipment for a fifteenth-century mariner, as depicted in a work by the Venetian cartographer Andrea Bianco.

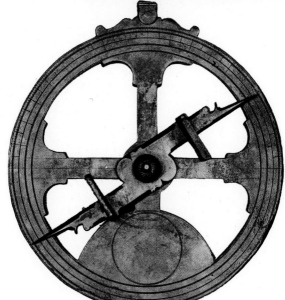

Above, a model of the Santa Maria, the largest of the three ships on Columbus' maiden voyage to America. In debt and virtually forgotten, Columbus died in 1506 and was interred in the cathedral at Seville in 1509. His remains were later removed to Hispaniola and then to Cuba, only to be returned to Seville in 1899. Below, sculptures from the explorer's tomb in the cathedral of Seville.

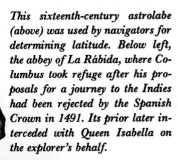

This sixteenth-century astrolabe (above) was used by navigators for determining latitude. Below left, the abbey of La Rábida, where Columbus took refuge after his proposals for a journey to the Indies had been rejected by the Spanish Crown in 1491. Its prior later interceded with Queen Isabella on the explorer's behalf.

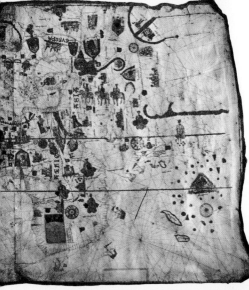

liked. It soon became obvious to Charles' advisers that the presence of Ferdinand in Spain could do their master no good, and so Charles' brother was sent off to the Netherlands on the pretext that travel would further his education.

A few years later, Charles delegated to this amiable young man the delicate task of governing the Hapsburg possessions in Austria. Ferdinand, the "Spanish brother," soon became as well adapted to his new surroundings as he had once been to those in Madrid. Although not destined to play any further role in the affairs of the Spanish monarchy, Ferdinand became the founder of the Austrian branch of the Hapsburg family.

Ferdinand's departure from Spain did not end resistance to the Flemish-reared Charles. The nobility and towns of the Spanish kingdoms and provinces had accepted the unified monarchy of Ferdinand and Isabella because it was identified with the crusade to drive non-Christian powers from the Iberian Peninsula. The prospect of a foreigner on the throne, especially one who might well be absent from the country for years at a time, was a different matter entirely.

When the Castilian Cortes (parliament) met to swear its oath of allegiance to the new king, it made no attempt to conceal its loyalties to Juana la Loca, who was technically still coruler with Charles. The Cortes of Aragon was even more obstinate, forcing Charles to dismiss one of his Burgundian advisers, the hated Jean de Sauvage, to gain its loyalty. The worst fears that Charles would be an absentee king were confirmed when word was received that the young monarch had been elected to succeed his grandfather as Holy Roman emperor. As the ultimate insult, monies voted by the Cortes of Castile were to be used to pay for the king's journey to Germany.

Although Charles I of Spain was now entitled to call himself Charles V, Holy Roman emperor, the price of this newly acquired grandeur was the division of Spain into bitterly opposed factions for and against the monarchy. Soon after Charles left the country in May 1520, a wave of violence swept through the towns of Castile as supporters of the guilds and urban communes took up arms to defend their traditional privileges against the demands of the king's advisers. The Castilian rebellion, known as the Communero Revolt, was one of the largest uprisings in Spanish history. From the beginning, resentment was focused on foreigners, especially Adrian of Utrecht, the regent of Castile. The Castilian aristocracy at first did nothing to check the spread of the movement, whose supporters looked back nostalgically to the time of Ferdinand and Isabella. When the insurgence took on the dimensions of a more sweeping social protest,

20

The marriage in 1496 of Philip the Handsome, archduke of Austria (top right), to the infanta Juana (center right) united Hapsburg and Spanish domains. Juana, driven mad by her husband's death in 1506, spent the last forty-six years of her life in a small, windowless cell in the convent of Santa Clara at Tordesillas (left). Although she was titular queen of Castile, the real power was held by her father, Ferdinand, and later by her son Charles (bottom right), who was named co-monarch in 1516.

Below, the children of Juana and Philip, as portrayed in a diptych by an unknown Flemish artist in the early sixteenth century. The sons, Ferdinand and Charles, are depicted on the left panel. On the right panel are the four daughters: Leonora, later married to Emanuel the Great of Portugal and Francis I of France; Isabella, who wed Christian II of Denmark; Mary, who was to become the queen of Louis II of Hungary and regent of the Netherlands; and Catherine, who later married the Portuguese king John III.

THE SPANISH KINGDOM

Spain and the Hapsburgs

Boundaries of the domain of Charles V

Heritage of Philip II

Territories controlled by the Kingdom of Spain in 1648

The empire of the Spanish Hapsburgs emerged in the fifteenth century, during a transitional era in European history. At the time, the feudal order was dying, and both France and England were torn by the quarrels of their great noble families. Burgundy, which had appeared destined to become a major power, was stymied by the defeat of Charles the Bold in 1477. A new system of nation states was developing, in which monarchs claimed the right to control a centralized administration, raise national armies, and impose taxes on a regular basis.

In Spain, the numerous kingdoms of the medieval period had already come under the rule of Castile and Aragon, which were united in 1479, ten years after the marriage of Ferdinand of Aragon and Isabella of Castile. The conquest of the Moorish kingdom of Granada in 1492 completed the formation of the modern Spanish state. Regional feelings remained strong, however, and the old kingdoms retained distinct political identities.

Charles, Ferdinand and Isabella's Flemish grandson, ascended the Spanish throne in 1516 and three years later became Holy Roman Emperor Charles V. His domains included Spain and its Italian possessions (Naples, Sicily, and Sardinia), as well as the Burgundian lands that he had inherited through his father, Philip (territory in the Low Countries and the Franche-Comté, a region just west of present-day Switzerland). The duchy of Milan,

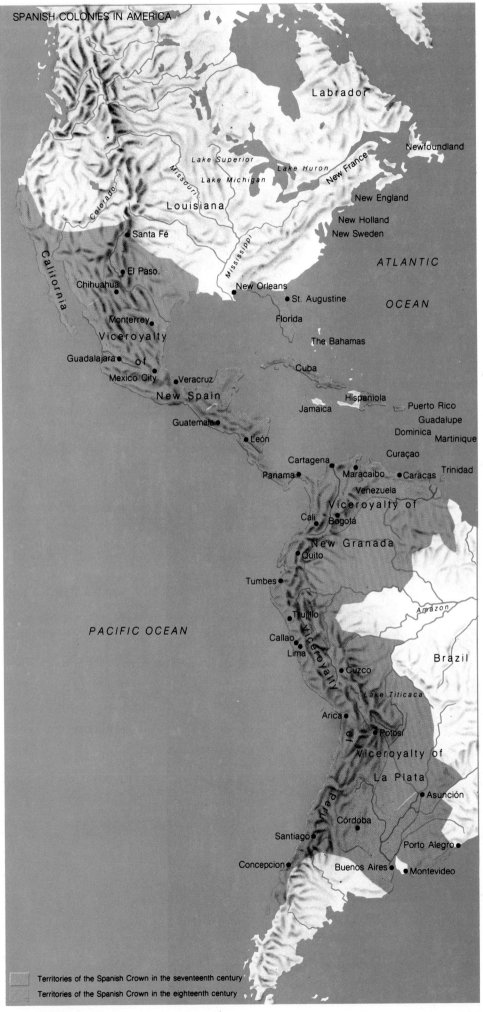

taken from the French in 1526, added to this string of rich possessions along the spine of western Europe. A large part of Charles V's dominions, however—the Holy Roman Empire and the Hapsburg lands in Austria, the Tyrolean region, and the Rhine area—proved impossible to control and was severed from the inheritance of Charles' son, Philip II of Spain.

The Protestant Reformation, which erupted in Germany in the sixteenth century, eventually led to the Thirty Years' War and the Peace of Westphalia (1648). As part of this agreement, the Spanish Hapsburgs, who had come to the aid of their Austrian cousins, were forced to concede the independence of the United Provinces of Holland. Nonetheless, they still enjoyed a commanding strategic postition in Europe.

By 1713, the transitional period that had seen the rise of the Hapsburgs was over. England, France, and Austria had survived internal crises and emerged as the dominant powers of Europe. In the War of the Spanish Succession they fought over the throne left vacant by the childless Charles II, the last Spanish Hapsburg. Spain survived as a nation but had to accept a ruler from the French House of Bourbon.

In spite of Spain's declining fortunes, the Spanish territories in the New World managed to preserve their integrity and even to expand. Spain's colonies stood staunchly opposed to any plan of partition among the European powers, and in the eighteenth century this tenacity was rewarded with the creation of two new South American viceroyalties—New Granada and La Plata—and the establishment of Spanish military governments in Texas and California.

The Alcántara Bridge (above) in Toledo dates from Roman times but has been repeatedly restored.

Below, Charles V, in a portrait by Juan Pantoja de la Cruz, the official court painter at the time of Philip II.

however, the nobility quickly decided that its interests lay with the Hapsburg king. By the end of 1521 the rebellion had been quashed, and Castilian society was forced to begin viewing itself as a part of Europe, culturally and politically.

When he first arrived in Germany as Holy Roman emperor, Charles was welcomed by the imperial electors. (It was no secret that Charles owed his title to his ability to outbribe the other candidates for the imperial crown, notably Francis I of France and Henry VIII of England.) Relations soured, though, when the electors discovered that they had been wrong in thinking Charles a fellow German: The new emperor, educated in French-speaking Ghent, was no more German than he was Spanish. Worse still, Charles was soon seen to be unequal to the task of preventing a major religious division within the empire.

The first act of the German drama was played out in the city of Worms in the spring of 1521, while Charles was presiding over a session of the imperial diet. Through the influence of some of the diet's members, the contumacious monk Martin Luther had been ordered to appear and explain his religious teachings. Knowing that some of Charles' closest advisers admired the reformist writings of the Dutch theologian Erasmus, Luther and his supporters had reason to believe that the emperor would give their ideas a fair hearing. They even thought that Charles could be convinced to take up the cause of reforming the Church. These expectations did not, however, take into account Charles' position as ruler of Catholic Spain, Burgundy, Naples, and Sicily. Spain in particular could never be expected to reconcile itself to a king who lent his support to a notorious German heretic.

Summoned before the diet, Luther was prepared for a debate; he was instead given twenty-four hours to recant his position. Luther firmly refused to retreat from his beliefs. Only an imperial safe conduct issued for Luther's appearance at Worms stood between the outlawed monk and execution. As he departed the convocation in a rickety ox cart, Luther was set upon by kidnapers in the employ of the elector of Saxony, who spirited him away to Wartburg Castle—not for imprisonment but for his own protection. The very development Charles most sought to avoid was occurring: Lutheranism had ceased to be a set of ideas and was becoming a movement, one that would eventually lead to a deep rift in Germany.

Charles' early experiences in Spain and Germany forcefully demonstrated the obstacles that kept his personal inheritance from becoming a true Hapsburg empire. Each subject territory had its own customs

During Charles V's visit to Brussels in 1531, the guild of merchants presented the emperor with seven tapestries depicting scenes from the battle fought between the Hapsburgs and the French at Pavia, Italy, in 1525. Above, the French assault. Right, the capture of Francis I of France by the more powerful Hapsburg army. Below, an anonymous portrait of Francis I.

and traditions and strongly resented the prospect of sacrificing its native institutions for the development of an integrated bureaucracy. Charles, who thought of his domains as a personal legacy, shared this point of view to an extent. When it became clear that he could not oversee all his lands at once, Charles delegated power to members of his immediate family: His aunt was made regent of the Netherlands (she was later succeeded by Charles' sister); Ferdinand, his brother, was given authority in Austria; and Isabella of Portugal, his wife, became regent of Spain during the emperor's absences from that country.

Warfare

The reign of Charles V coincided with a period in which the art of warfare was revolutionized. Artillery had been in use for some time prior to this era. The Ottoman Turks, for example, had used large cannons in their assault on Constantinople in 1453. The appearance of Spanish harquebusiers in the battle of Bicocca in 1522 marked, however, the first time that portable weapons played a decisive role in a European engagement. The harquebusiers fought in three lines, with those in the front line resting their harquebuses (heavy matchlock guns) on forked sticks to fire and then moving to the rear to reload.

The introduction of portable firearms rendered the heavily armed knight obsolete. The knights, who fought for glory, plunder, and ransom money, were replaced by trained mercenary soldiers, whose loyalty was contingent on their receiving regular wages. Little wonder that medieval cavalrymen scorned firearms and that the Italian poet Lodovico Ariosto dubbed these weapons an "ugly, wicked invention." Success in battle was coming to have less to do with skill or gallantry and more to do with finances.

Above, various types of mortars, which were used as siege weapons during the sixteenth century. Left, two falconets, light artillery pieces with an estimated range of two miles.

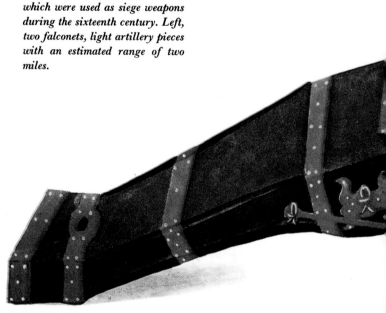

Above, a glass hand grenade. The first grenades, dating from the fifteenth century, were made of earthenware filled with gunpowder. Glass and metal versions appeared later. Below, a medium-caliber piece of artillery. From the second half of the sixteenth century, all artillery was muzzle-loaded.

Above, harquebuses and their use. The first harquebuses were two-man weapons fired from portable tripods. The process of positioning and firing these guns took five minutes.

Precisely because the Hapsburg "empire" never amounted to more than an aggregation of separate kingdoms, it was necessary for Charles to develop a coherent philosophy of his role as monarch. Mercurino Gattinara, a lawyer and scholar who served as Charles' chancellor, was largely responsible for the emperor's decision to take Charlemagne as his model. As the secular champion of Christendom, Charles hoped to lead Europe against the infidel Turks and the heretical Protestants and to usher in an era of "one emperor and one universal law." If the monarchs of Europe could be persuaded to put aside their petty quarrels and unite against Islam, Charles reasoned, Christendom could be unified and the Church purified from within.

Charles' grand plan was totally unrealistic. Much of Europe was more interested in fighting Charles than in crusading against the Turks, and Christian unity was already irretrievably lost. The aspiration to become a "universal emperor" did, however, have a beneficial effect on Charles' character. The inexperienced and freakish-looking youth who had so dismayed his Spanish subjects in 1517 began maturing into a figure who commanded respect and admiration. A diligent worker who seldom spared himself the rigors of long hours and arduous travel, Charles taught himself the habit of command.

In 1521, conflicting claims in Burgundy led to the beginning of a protracted struggle between Charles and Francis I of France. Francis, who had grown up in a court that clung to the traditions of chivalry, fancied himself something of a medieval knight. Although his nocturnal escapades were notorious, the tall, lanky Francis could be impeccably charming and courteous when the occasion called for it. In matters of state he was inclined to follow his own whims.

Italy was destined to be the battleground between Charles and Francis. Having begun his reign in 1515 with a victorious campaign in northern Italy, Francis could never reconcile himself to the subsequent recapture of Milan by a Hapsburg army in 1522. Three years later he led an army across the Alps only to be captured by Charles at Pavia in Italy and carried off as a prisoner to Madrid. After extended negotiations, Francis signed the Treaty of Madrid, a pact he had no intention of honoring. He went through with his agreement to marry Charles' sister Eleanor but scandalized everyone by appearing at a window with his mistress to watch his bride's entry into Paris. By mid-1526, Francis had formed a new alliance with the pope and the rulers of Venice and Milan and was preparing for another Italian campaign.

The French-Hapsburg wars in Italy were sordid and ruinously expensive affairs that shed little glory

Above, a nautical map of 1571 showing Spain and the North African coast. In 1538, Charles V, the pope, and the rulers of Venice organized a combined fleet of one hundred and forty galleys under Gian Andrea Doria to attack the North African pirate Barbarossa Khair ed-Din, who had recently been made supreme commander of the Turkish fleet. An attack on the Turks at Preveza (in western Greece) ended in disaster, however, because of disputes among the allies. Right, the battle of Preveza.

Titian's painting of Emperor Charles V in full armor (right) was executed to commemorate the imperial victory over the Schmalkaldic League at Mühlberg in 1547. Titian captured the steadiness and determination of the mature Charles and, in the swirling clouds behind, a hint of impending tragedy. (The pose echoes that of a famous equestrian statue of the Roman emperor Marcus Aurelius which was believed at the time to represent Constantine the Great.)

Below, a scene from a tapestry depicting the battle of Mühlberg.

on any of the participants. Francis elected to conduct clandestine negotiations with the Turks, and two of the leading French commanders, the duke of Bourbon and the Genoese admiral Andrea Doria, defected to the Hapsburg side. In 1527 the conflict reached its nadir when imperial troops, many of them Lutheran mercenaries from Germany, marched on Rome, sacking the city and besieging the pope in the Castel Sant'Angelo. By 1529 the exhausted French were ready to sign a treaty in earnest. When Charles, a year later, decided to celebrate his long-delayed coronation as Holy Roman emperor, he was forced to hold the ceremony in Bologna: Rome, the city the

emperor was theoretically to champion and defend, had been devastated by his own army.

With the signing of the Peace of Cambrai in 1529, Charles was at last free to turn his attention to the Turks, whom he had long considered his deadliest enemies. The opportunity came none too soon, for the Turks menaced European security on a number of fronts. In 1526 a Turkish army had defeated and killed the king of Hungary at Mohács; the Hapsburg capital of Vienna was threatened; and the Christian-born pirate Barbarossa Khair ed-Din had captured Algiers and was launching raids on the Spanish coast of the Mediterranean. For once, Charles was about to

Antonio de Mendoza (upper left) was named viceroy of New Spain in 1535 and viceroy of Peru in 1550. The New World viceroyalties, along with seven others, were created to administer the possessions of the Crown of Aragon. Immediately above, the reverse of one of the first coins minted in Mexico by the Spanish conquerors. Right, a map drawn in the second half of the sixteenth century, revealing a fairly extensive knowledge of coastal waters and the Amazon Valley.

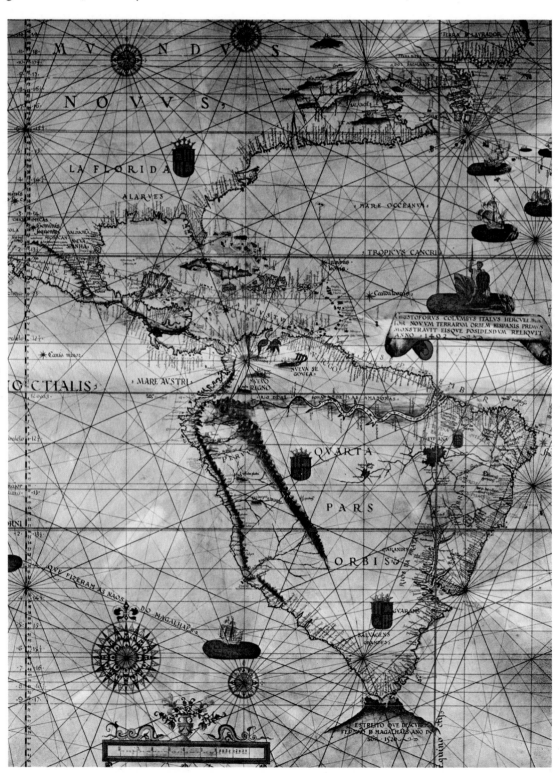

fight a war that was popular with his Spanish subjects (who paid the greatest part of the costs)—and even the princes of Germany were moved to help raise a great army for the relief of Vienna.

The threat of Hapsburg retaliation proved enough to drive the Turks from the Danube without a battle in 1532. Three years later, Charles enjoyed a hard-fought—and therefore more satisfying—victory when a fleet of more than four hundred ships seized the North African port of Tunis, expelling Barbarossa and his Turkish naval force. The triumph at Tunis was the high point of Charles' career. He began then to contemplate taking the port of Algiers, where Bar-

barossa and his ships had sought refuge.

It did not take long for Charles to discover that the capture of Tunis represented a climax rather than a beginning. The death of the duke of Milan that same year touched off another expensive and distracting round of conflict with France, making it impossible for Charles to continue his Mediterranean campaign. In Germany, Charles was forced to address himself to an even more ominous situation: The founding of the Schmalkaldic League in 1531 had signaled the willingness of Protestant princes and towns to defend themselves against imperial authority by force of arms. It was 1541 before Charles had a chance to

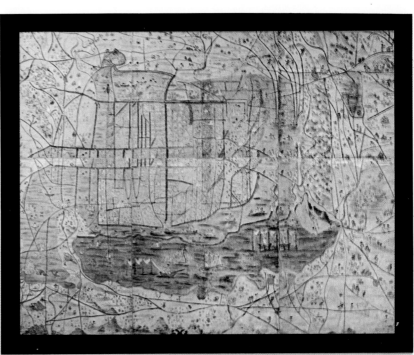

Above, Christoph Fugger, in a 1541 portrait by Christoph Amberger. As a result of their substantial loans to the House of Hapsburgs, the Fuggers, a family of financiers and merchants, controlled the income from the silver mines of the Tyrolean region and the copper mines of Hungary.

Above right, a map of colonial Mexico City, executed in Madrid in 1628. Near right, an Aztec in ceremonial dress, as illustrated in Bernardino de Sahagún's General History of the Things of New Spain. *The Dominican friar Bartolomé de Las Casas (far right) stirred controversy in Spain by protesting the enslavement and forced conversion of the Indian population.*

The Codex Mendoza

In the century after the conquest of Mexico, the Indians of the New World became pawns in a struggle between the Spanish colonists, who wanted to exploit native labor for the benefit of their private fortunes, and the missionaries and representatives of the Crown, who hoped that the Indians could be assimilated as Christian subjects of the Spanish king. Although the possibility of allowing the Indians to retain their own religions and institutions was never seriously considered, there were Spaniards who took a scholarly interest in preserving data about the history of the Aztec Empire and the customs of Indian society before the arrival of the Europeans.

One of the best extant sources of information is the Codex Mendoza, which is

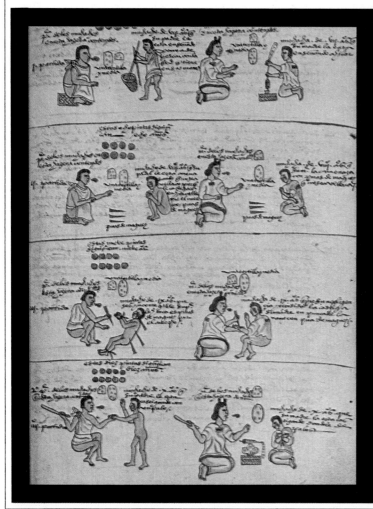

named after the viceroy who sent the manuscript from Mexico as a gift to the emperor Charles V in 1549. (It is now kept in Oxford University's Bodleian Library.) Written in Spanish and Aztec, the codex contains a history of the Aztecs from the founding of the city of Tenochtitlán to 1520, a reproduction of a "book of taxes," and a description of Aztec customs.

These pages, illustrations from the Codex Mendoza. Above (left to right), an eagle perched on a prickly-pear cactus—the symbol of Tenochtitlán; a shell drawing from a "book of taxes" signifying that a payment had been made; five- and six-year-old boys being trained to take goods to market; a symbolic representation of a king burning a temple and imposing taxes on the conquered; and a child's naming ceremony. Facing page, below, scenes depicting the education and disciplining of children. This page, below (counter-

clockwise from upper left), a bride being carried to her husband's home; a wedding ceremony; and a representation of a priest and a secular teacher of martial arts.

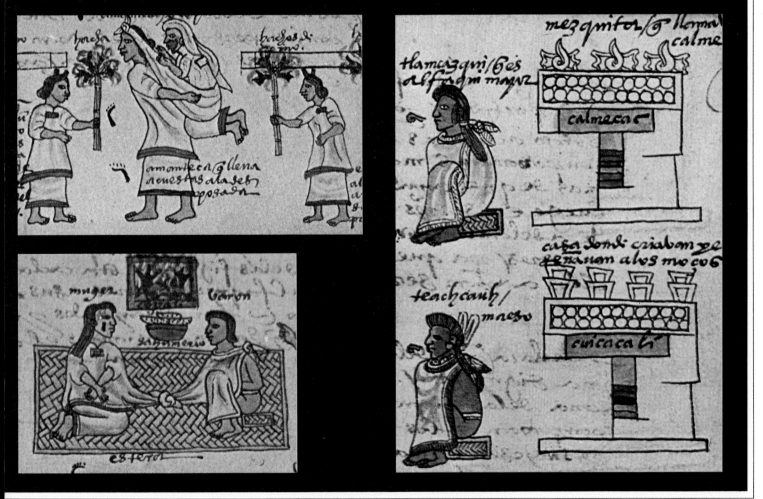

launch a follow-up expedition against Algiers, long after the momentum of the Tunis campaign had dissipated. Plagued by storms and miscalculations, the Algerian campaign foundered—and with it, Charles' image as the crusading champion of Christendom.

While Charles was pursuing his expensive and often inconclusive wars on the Continent, he became, through no effort of his own, master of an empire even larger than the one he had inherited: New Spain. There is no evidence that Charles ever came to appreciate the revolutionary significance of the accomplishments of Hernando Cortés, Francisco Pizarro, and the other conquistadors; his memoirs do not even mention the voyages. But the impact on Castile, whose Crown controlled the new lands by virtue of Columbus' commission from Ferdinand and Isabella, was immediate and dramatic. The crusading tradition that had lain dormant since medieval times (when campaigns were launched to end the Moorish occupation of the Iberian Peninsula) found a new outlet, and the sons of the *hidalguía,* or lesser nobility, seized on the opportunity to exercise the military skills for which their education and class background had prepared them. In addition, the influx of gold and silver from the mines of the New World, combined with the creation of a vast new market for Spanish goods, sparked the development of entire new industries, especially textile manufacturing.

Many of the Spanish churchmen who accompanied the conquistadors to the New World returned home filled with indignation at what they had seen, especially the *encomienda* system, which in effect permitted individual colonists to exploit the forced labor of the native populations. The Church—and all of educated Spain—was shaken by the debate between those who argued that the enslavement and forcible conversion of the Indians was morally justifiable and those, like Bishop Bartolomé de Las Casas, who held that the Indians were subjects of the Crown and thus entitled to its protection.

Las Casas, known to later generations as the "Apostle of the Indians," was an outspoken opponent of the encomienda system. Arriving in the New World for the first time in 1502, Las Casas worked to convert Indians to Christianity and took part in colonizing expeditions. Increasingly appalled by the decimation of native populations, he returned to Spain in 1515 to plead for the reform of exploitative practices. In a speech before the Spanish Parliament in 1519, Las Casas convinced Charles to approve the alternate plan of forming "towns of free Indians"—communities of Spaniards and Indians who would jointly create a new civilization in America. The

Although Charles V never established a permanent capital, he commissioned the brilliant architect Alonso de Covarrubias to transform Toledo into a suitably dignified imperial seat. Left, Covarrubias' Puerta Nueva de Bisagra. Charles V's palace at Granada (above), begun in 1528, was among the first buildings in Spain designed in the Italian Renaissance style.

While in residence at Augsburg (in the south of present-day Germany) in 1548, Titian executed portraits of Queen Isabella and Charles V (below). Although at the time the queen had been dead for almost ten years, Titian captured the youthful beauty of Isabella, who remained alive in Charles' affections.

Don Quixote

The conflict between the flesh and the spirit and between the real and the ideal dominated the consciousness of Spanish writers during the fifteenth and sixteenth centuries. None handled this theme with greater wit and humanity than Miguel de Cervantes Saavedra.

Cervantes' novel *Don Quixote* is a satire—not of the values of chivalry per se, but of the pretensions of an impoverished middle-aged *hidalgo* (member of the lesser nobility) who imagines himself to be a knight errant. Cervantes knew from experience that the values celebrated in the chivalric romances of his day were seldom rewarded in practice. Forced to flee the country after a duel, the writer later served valorously at the battle of Lepanto and survived five years as a captive of the Barbary pirates, leading four unsuccessful escape attempts before he was ransomed. After this dashing career, he returned home to the life of an impecunious poet and minor bureaucrat.

When Part I of *Don Quixote* was published in 1605, readers from Madrid to the farthest reaches of Spain's New World empire recognized something of themselves in the deluded knight. In Part II of the story the don becomes a true split personality, able to meet and admire himself as a fictional hero. Ironically, although the book was an immediate popular success, it brought Cervantes neither riches nor the critical recognition he had longed for. It was not until the present century that the philosophic implications of the book were acknowledged.

One of Don Quixote's most memorable adventures takes place when the hero mistakes windmills for giants and attempts to engage them in combat. These windmills (above left) are in the same region as La Mancha, Don Quixote's birthplace. Immediately above, a depiction of Don Quixote (right) and Sancho Panza, his pragmatic squire (left). Top, the house in the city of Valladolid where Cervantes lived in 1605; the building is today a museum.

model town—Cumuná—proved to be a failure, and in 1523 a discouraged Las Casas abandoned his reforming activities to retire to a convent where he wrote the *Historia de las Indias.* In this volume Las Casas predicted Spain's downfall, which he attributed to the gold-greediness of Spanish colonists in the New World. In 1544, at Las Casas' prompting, Charles signed the so-called New Laws, which forbade abuses of the encomienda system and specifically abolished hereditary privilege in the colonies. Las Casas, as bishop of Chiapas in Guatemala, was sent to enforce these laws. Returning to Spain in 1547, Las Casas became embroiled in an argument with Juan Ginés de Sepúlvedra, who believed Indians were biologically inferior. Comparing Indians to white men, he argued, was like comparing apes, or women, to men. They were not equals; hence Indians could legitimately be enslaved. The debate raged in the Spanish court for years.

The difficult decision by Charles and his ministers to prohibit slavery among the Indian population was based partly on humanitarian considerations and partly on the desire to inhibit the growth of a powerful hereditary aristocracy in the new colonies. The establishment of viceroyalties in the New World and the promulgation of a reformed legal code in 1542 came too late to prevent the horrible abuses that decimated the Indian population, nor did they alter the fact that profits from the colonies were inevitably dependent on exploitation in one form or another. Nevertheless, the Crown's policy was a relatively enlightened one for its time, and the debate that shaped

As part of a general reorganization of the Spanish government, Francisco de los Cobos, Charles V's secretary, established a state archives at the castle of Simancas (above left). Cobos laid the foundations for the bureaucracy that Philip II was later to rely on. Above, an elaborately sculpted window in the palace where Philip II was born in 1527. Below, the youthful Philip, as painted by Anthony More.

The character of Philip II

Philip II lived all his life in the shadow of his father, Charles V. Like many sons of legendary personalities, Philip was burdened by the feeling that he could never measure up to his father's example. Lacking confidence in his own impulses, he took refuge in a rigid adherence to principle. In some respects, the results were admirable. Philip's devotion to justice, for example, and his refusal to tamper with the courts earned the king widespread respect. Philip's insecurity made him vulnerable, however, to plotters like Antonio Pérez, who used his favored position as the king's secretary to sell state secrets, arrange the assassination of a rival courtier, and scheme against the Crown's interests in the Portuguese succession.

Always more comfortable with paperwork than with other human beings, Philip found little respite from loneliness in his personal life. He survived four wives and was a distant father to all his children, except his daughters by Elizabeth of Valois, whom he treated affectionately.

Above, Philip's private apartment in the Escorial. The king's suite consisted of three sparsely furnished rooms occupying a total area of about ninety square yards.

Anna of Austria (left) was the daughter of Maximilian II, the Holy Roman emperor. In 1570 she became Philip's fourth wife. Elizabeth of Valois (right) was sixteen when she became Philip's third wife.

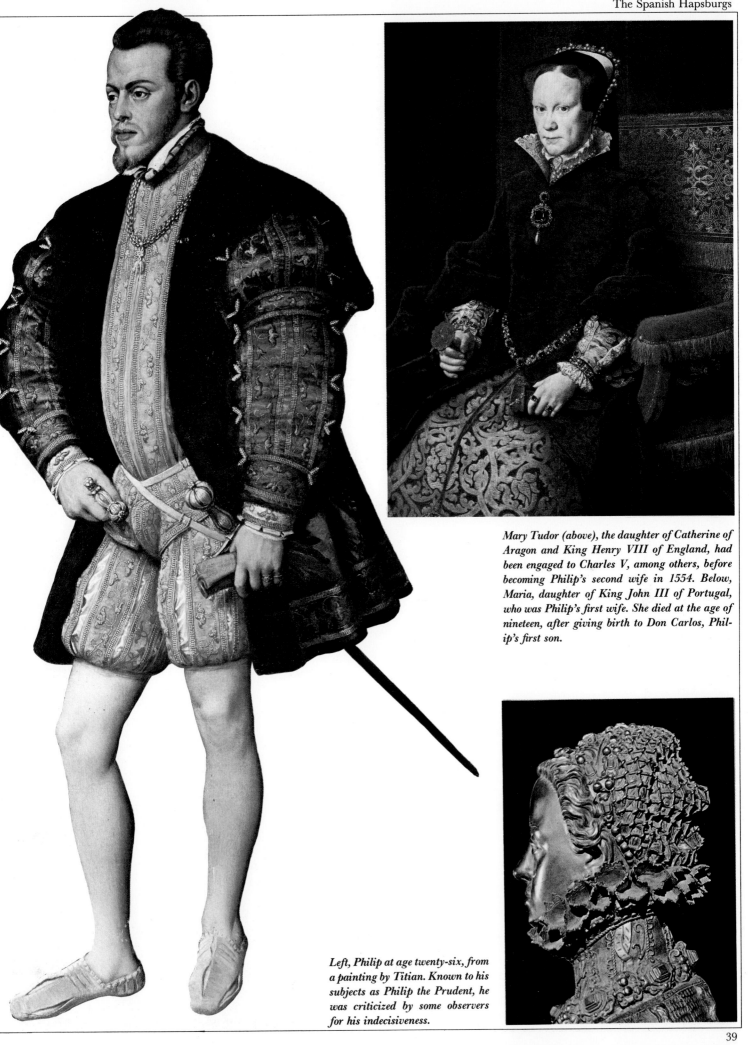

Mary Tudor (above), the daughter of Catherine of Aragon and King Henry VIII of England, had been engaged to Charles V, among others, before becoming Philip's second wife in 1554. Below, Maria, daughter of King John III of Portugal, who was Philip's first wife. She died at the age of nineteen, after giving birth to Don Carlos, Philip's first son.

Left, Philip at age twenty-six, from a painting by Titian. Known to his subjects as Philip the Prudent, he was criticized by some observers for his indecisiveness.

This fresco (left) in the Escorial's Hall of Battles commemorates Spain's victory over France in the battle of Saint-Quentin, fought in August 1557. Above, a fresco, also from the Hall of Battles, depicting Gravelines, where the forces of Henry II of France were beaten in 1558 by a Spanish army led by the count of Egmont.

it testified to the intellectual and moral vitality of Castilian society.

Charles viewed his New World colonies primarily as a convenient source of income that would enable him to pursue the goals he considered most important, including the destruction of the Schmalkaldic League. Charles deliberately maneuvered the Schmalkaldic League into a war, having first neutralized the league's leader, Philip of Hesse, by threatening prosecution for a bigamous marriage Philip had contracted. After the decisive imperial victory over the league at the battle of Mühlberg in 1547, the

emperor imposed what he hoped would be a final settlement to the religious issue smoldering in Germany—an agreement that made minor concessions to the Lutherans but none at all to the recently emerged Calvinists. By then, however, the religious and political situation in Germany had deteriorated irremediably. The Council of Trent, convened in 1545 at Charles' urging, proved incapable of resolving pressing religious issues. In addition, the German princes, regardless of their religion, were growing increasingly confident of their ability to defy and resist imperial authority.

As the 1540s drew to a close, Charles was an ill and

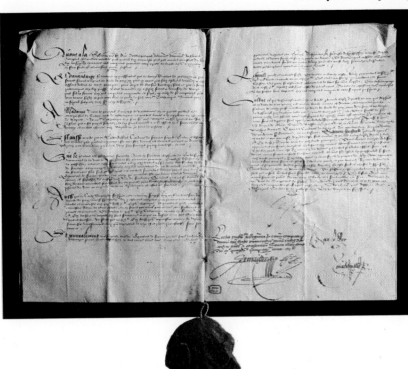

The Treaty of Cateau-Cambrésis (above) was a decisive blow to French ambitions in Italy. "By a stroke of the pen," wrote one Frenchman, "all our conquests of thirty years have been handed back."

Left, a painting that represents the Treaty of Cateau-Cambrésis as a symbolic embrace between the sovereigns of Spain and France. In reality, neither Philip II nor Henry II attended the peace conference. Following pages, the expulsion of the Moriscos from Spain in 1609–1610, from an unpublished drawing by Vincente Carducho in the collection of Madrid's Prado Museum.

prematurely aged man. His great opponents, Francis I and Martin Luther, were dead; the era when the Lutherans of Germany might have accepted a reconciliation with the Church had passed; and even Ferdinand, his loyal brother, was beginning to act on the assumption that Charles would never be able to reunite the empire. Maurice, the elector of Saxony—a Protestant who had been one of Charles' most effective supporters—finally concluded that the time had come to chart his own course. In 1552, Maurice's army surprised Charles at the city of Innsbruck, and the emperor was forced to flee over the Brenner Pass to Carinthia (in the south of present-day Austria).

Three years later, in September 1555, the Peace of Augsburg was promulgated, permitting each German prince and free imperial city to choose between Catholicism and Lutheranism. Charles, refusing to accept the inevitability of this agreement and thus the collapse of his entire German policy, decided to abdicate in favor of his son, Philip. His own disappointment was matched by regrets for his son, who had no hope of succeeding him as Holy Roman emperor: Charles' brother Ferdinand had already declared his intention to take the title, thus excluding Philip from the Hapsburg inheritance in Austria.

To make sure that the transfer of power in the

Lepanto

Early Turkish advances on the Danube and in the Mediterranean aroused fears that the entire European continent would be overwhelmed by a Moslem tide. Alarmed by Turkish assaults on Malta and Cyprus, Spain and Venice finally overcame their mutual distrust and in 1571 dispatched a joint fleet under the command of Don John of Austria. The allies were fortunate enough to surprise the entire Turkish fleet in the Bay of Lepanto, off the coast of Greece, and in three hours of fierce fighting destroyed virtually the entire Turkish navy and liberated more than ten thousand Christian galley slaves. The battle, fought on October 9, was the last great sea engagement between oar-powered galleys.

The allies failed to press their advantage after the victory at Lepanto, however, allowing the Turks to rebuild their fleet. The strategic stalemate in the Mediterranean thus continued.

Don John of Austria (above), the hero of Lepanto, was an illegitimate son of Charles V. He dreamed of carving an empire for himself out of lands liberated from the Turks and later planned to invade England, which he intended to rule as the husband of Mary Stuart. Neither of these schemes succeeded.

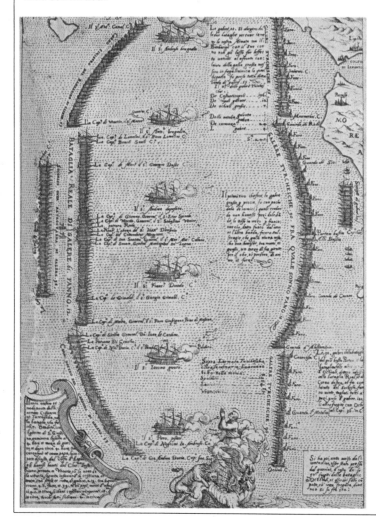

At Lepanto (above) enemy ships were boarded for fierce hand-to-hand combat. The development of more maneuverable vessels and longer-range artillery was soon to make floating garrisons like the great Venetian galleass (right) obsolete. Far left, a chart showing the positions of the opposing fleets at the beginning of the battle. The Turkish vessels are on the right, and those of the Holy League, primarily Venetian and Spanish ships, are on the left. Agustín Barbarigo (near left), commander of the Venetian contingent, was killed during the fighting. The Venetians blamed his death on the treachery of the Genoese admiral Andrea Doria, who fought under the auspices of the Spanish.

Netherlands went smoothly, Charles arranged to hand over the reins of government personally. On October 25, 1555, in a tearful ceremony at the ducal palace in Brussels, he delivered a moving farewell. "Nine times I have been to Germany, six to Spain, seven to Italy, ten times here to Flanders, four times in peace and war I have entered France, twice I have visited England and on two other occasions I went to Africa. . . . If I give way to tears, gentlemen, do not believe it is on account of the sovereignty of which I am stripping myself at this moment. It is because I must leave the country of my birth and say farewell to such lieges as I have here."

Charles spent the last two years of his life in Spain, a country he had belatedly come to regard as his home. He lived quietly, enjoying unaccustomed luxury and the rich foods he had always loved. Although

crippled by gout, he refused to make any concessions to his disease—just as he had refused to bow before the historical forces that were destroying the old order he represented.

As long as he was physically able, Charles V had governed his empire from the saddle. By contrast, Philip II, his son, preferred to rule from behind a desk. Philip, who served as his own chief minister, dutifully read and considered every document that came his way from the sizable bureaucracy created during Charles' reign. Boldness, however, was not in his nature, and the flood of petitions produced only a trickle of decisions in return. Philip's Castilian subjects called him *el rey papelero* ("the paperwork king"), and the rest of Europe, Hapsburg domains included, saw him as a distant and forbidding figure. In the

Left, ships of the Spanish Armada before their departure from the port of Lisbon. Although the English were initially disappointed by their failure to destroy the entire Armada in 1588, England's victory later became a source of patriotic inspiration. Paintings in the National Maritime Museum in Greenwich, England, recall the encounter of the two fleets (below) and an engagement between two vessels (right).

words of one ambassador: "The Italians did not like him much, the Flemings not at all, and the Germans found him odious."

Philip's youthful experiences did little to lighten a naturally somber nature. A widower at twenty-one, he was sent to England to marry his father's cousin Mary Tudor and father an heir who might unite England and Spain. The English, however, were not at all disposed to welcome a Spanish prince. When Philip closed the doors of his private quarters, seeking the seclusion that was in his homeland considered appropriate, the English suspected him of plotting a revolt. And when he retired to the Netherlands to indulge in a spell of philandering, the English were as offended as their abandoned queen.

In 1558 the emperor Charles and Mary Tudor died within a few months of each other, leaving Philip free to return to Spain and the privacy he craved. Spain at the time was caught up in a mood of religious zealotry. Rumors of Protestant infiltration had inspired the Inquisition (an ecclesiastical tribunal established in the late fifteenth century to combat heresy) to issue a series of stringent censorship decrees, and by 1559 a full-scale campaign was under way to ferret out and destroy banned books. Swayed by antiforeign feeling and the fear of heresy, Philip became so fervently orthodox that he did not even trust the pope to uphold the Church's interests. Philip's militancy sprang partly from his rigid personality and partly from his appreciation of historical and geographical circumstances: Philip headed an empire that was staunchly Catholic at its center but threatened in the south by Islam and in the north by the rising tide of Calvinism.

Elizabeth I of England (above) pursued a cautious foreign policy and avoided costly foreign wars, but she encouraged the exploits of English explorers and buccaneers like Sir Martin Frobisher (above right) and Sir John Hawkins (below). A rear admiral during the Armada's defeat in 1588, Hawkins also smuggled slaves into Spanish colonies and raided with Sir Francis Drake.

The troubles that broke out in the Hapsburg-controlled Netherlands in the 1560s had to do more with national than religious divisions. The policies of Margaret of Parma, the Hapsburg regent, were viewed by local aristocrats as a threat to their traditional fortunes. Only a small minority of the population was Calvinist, and even noblemen like William of Orange, who had Protestant connections and no love for the arrogant ways of Margaret's chief adviser, Cardinal Granvelle, regarded the new religion with suspicion. But the presence of a Spanish garrison and (after 1556) the Jesuits created a situation in which the balance of peace was uneasily maintained, with religious and secular tensions each working hard to exacerbate the other.

Both Margaret's council of state and the aristocrats hoped to avoid open conflict over religion, but Philip II, living far from the Netherlands in a country where the principle of "one state, one religion" still seemed inviolable, was determined to impose the Inquisition on all his subjects. In the autumn of 1565 he wrote to Margaret, bidding her to enforce the strict penalties against heresy. Margaret was so unnerved by this communication that she kept it secret for more than a week. Once published, the decree provided a ready target for popular discontent. On April 5, 1566, a delegation of more than two hundred nobles, Catholic and Protestant alike, appeared in Brussels to pre-

Above, Elizabeth I addressing her victorious commanders after the dispersal of the Armada. A portion of the queen's eloquent speech is inscribed on the painting. Above center, English and Dutch ships attacking the Spanish.

sent their grievances and demand a cessation of the Inquisition's activities. When one of Margaret's advisers contemptuously dismissed the petitioners as mere "beggars," the nobles promptly adopted the name as a symbol of rebellion. By midsummer, unemployed and hungry workers were storming churches and destroying religious images, which were associated by the insurgents with the hated foreign clergy.

Some nobles, including William of Orange, were

sympathetic to the Beggars but reluctant to support open hostilities. Philip II, meanwhile, was torn between the counsel of those advocating moderation and the advice of the duke of Alva, one of his generals, who proposed quick and forceful suppression of the rebels. In the end, he decided to give Alva a free hand.

Alva arrived in the Netherlands in 1567 with an army nine thousand strong. His troops promptly set to work rounding up dissidents, beginning with the counts of Egmont and Horn, who were publicly executed in the Brussels market square. Over a six-year period, Alva's Council of Troubles returned some nine thousand guilty verdicts. More than a thousand persons were executed, and tens of thousands more fled the country.

In the short run, Alva's regime succeeded in scaring the people of the Netherlands into submission—indeed, it terrified all of Protestant Europe with the specter of an avenging anti-Protestant army. Gradually, however, outrage overcame fear. The common people expressed their resistance to Alva by steadfastly refusing to pay the new taxes he imposed, especially the "tenth penny," or ten percent sales tax. Those who had chosen exile flocked to the banner of William of Orange, who assumed the role of opposition leader. In 1572, Dutch rebels captured the port of Brielle. Although Alva contemptuously dismissed the event as signifying "nothing," the fall of Brielle was the beginning of the war that led to the establishment of the United Provinces of Holland.

In Iberia, too, Philip initiated a policy of repression. Here his wrath was directed against the Moriscos of Granada. Nominally Christian since 1499, the Moriscos spoke Arabic and dressed in Moorish styles. They were regarded as a racial as well as a religious minority and would hardly have been accepted by the Christian majority even if they had chosen to assimilate. Philip, fearing that the Morisco population would welcome a Turkish invasion, approved

Above left, William I, the founder of the Dutch Republic, as painted by Anthony More. A proud and complex man, William, prince of Orange, began his career as a loyal servant of the Hapsburgs. Later, as a leader of the Dutch rebels and as first stadholder (magistrate) of the Dutch Republic, he did much to foster a sense of national unity. After his assassination in 1584, William was eulogized as the father of his country. Left, Fernando Álvarez de Toledo, the duke of Alva, in a portrait by Titian. In his long career, Alva played an important role at the battle of Mühlberg and in the campaign leading to the annexation of Portugal in 1580–1581. He is best known for his suppression of the Netherlands revolt of 1567.

Above, the castle of Vianden in Luxembourg, the family seat of William I. Above right, a coin struck during the reign of Philip II. Below, proceedings before the Council of Troubles, a tribunal set up to prosecute Dutch rebels.

clumsy repressive measures that in time drove the Moriscos to outright rebellion against the state. For two years, Granada was torn by bitter and violent strife.

Because they were involved elsewhere, the ever-threatening Turks were not able to take full advan-

The Escorial

Philip II made Madrid the capital of his domains, but it was the Escorial, a vast fortress located some twenty-five miles outside the city, that expressed the spirit of his reign. In keeping with Philip's priorities, the Escorial was first a mausoleum for the kings of Spain, second a monastery and church for the Order of Saint Jerome, and third a royal palace.

The Escorial was begun to fulfill a vow Philip made in gratitude for his victory at the battle of Saint-Quentin in 1557 and was completed by 1584—a frantic pace by the standards of the time. Among the unusual features of this monastery-palace are the private apartments of the king and queen, which are located just behind the main altar of the church. A window opening from Philip's rooms into the sanctuary made it possible for the king to hear mass even when bedridden. In the last days of his life, Philip watched the rehearsals for his own funeral through this same window.

Above, a view of the Escorial as it appeared in the seventeenth century, by an unknown artist. The Escorial's architecture, an adaptation of the Italian Renaissance style, had enormous influence in Spain.

Left, the Hall of Battles, which contains a sixty-yard-long mural depicting the defeat inflicted in 1431 by John II, the king of Castile, on the Moors at Higueruela.

Right, a detail of the Escorial's facade, with a monumental statue of Saint Lawrence and Philip II's coat of arms. Below, the Escorial today. The monastery church attested to Philip's view of himself as "His Catholic Majesty" and the supreme defender of religious orthodoxy in Europe.

Left, gilded figures in bronze from the main chapel of the monastery church, representing (from left to right) Maria of Portugal, Elizabeth of Valois, Philip II, Don Carlos, and Anna of Austria. Below, the Pantheon of Kings, a crypt containing the remains of Spanish monarchs and their queens. Charles V and Philip II are interred here.

tage of the Granada rebellion to advance their own goals. In 1571, Spain joined with Venice and the Papal States to inflict a heavy blow to the Turks at Lepanto, off the coast of Greece. Although this naval victory was of little long-term practical significance, it had a decided impact on the morale of Christian Europe at that time.

Seven years after Lepanto, King Sebastian of Portugal, Philip's childless nephew, was killed in the course of a quixotic crusade against the Moors of North Africa. His death resulted in a substantial increase in the territory under Philip's sway. With the help of an army led by the duke of Alva, the Spanish

Above left, Philip II as he appeared shortly before his death. The portrait is by Philip's court painter, Juan Pantoja de la Cruz. Philip's daughter Isabella (top) was given the Netherlands and the Franche-Comté (in the east-central part of present-day France) as her dowry when she married Archduke Albert of Austria. As the marriage was childless, these lands were later reclaimed by Spain. Immediately above, Philip's son Don Carlos, who died in prison in 1568.

Above, the cloister of Santa Maria de Poblet, a monastery in Catalonia (northeastern Spain) founded by Cistercian monks in 1158. The monastery church was the burial place of the kings of Aragon and thus became for Catalan patriots a symbol of Aragonese and, later, Castilian domination. Burned during an anticlerical demonstration in 1835, it was subsequently restored.

king was able to convince the Portuguese of his right to the crown; in 1580, Philip became king of Portugal and won control of the Portuguese overseas empire.

For a time, the fortunes of Philip and Spain seemed on the rise. In the Netherlands, the governorship of Alessandro Farnese, Margaret of Parma's brilliant son, led to a more secure Spanish hold on the area. France, distracted by its own civil and religious wars, no longer posed a threat to Hapsburg ambitions. Increasingly, Philip's advisers were urging him to move against the one trouble spot that remained: England.

It had long been a cardinal principle of Spanish foreign policy to maintain good relations with England, if only to prevent the possibility of a French-English alliance. Yet ever since the ill-fated marriage of Catherine of Aragon to Henry VIII in 1509, Spain's dealings with the English Crown had never gone as planned. During his own unhappy marriage to Mary Tudor, Philip II had tried unsuccessfully to ingratiate himself with Elizabeth, her younger half sister. Although Protestant—and a daughter of Anne Boleyn, the woman whose name had become a synonym for whoredom throughout Castile—Elizabeth was still the most likely candidate to inherit the throne of England. Indeed, as Philip saw it, she was in some ways preferable to the Catholic Mary Stuart,

who was related to the duke of Guise and therefore likely to rule England in the interests of France if she became queen.

It was Elizabeth who in 1558 succeeded to the throne. The queen wasted no opportunity to try Philip's patience. She toyed with Philip's marriage proposal, meddled in the Netherlands revolt, and encouraged English privateers in their raids on Spanish shipping. Elizabeth did not relish the prospect of war any more than Philip did, however, and—skillful practitioner of the art of diplomatic ambiguity that she was—always managed to stop short of provoking an open confrontation.

The Holy Office

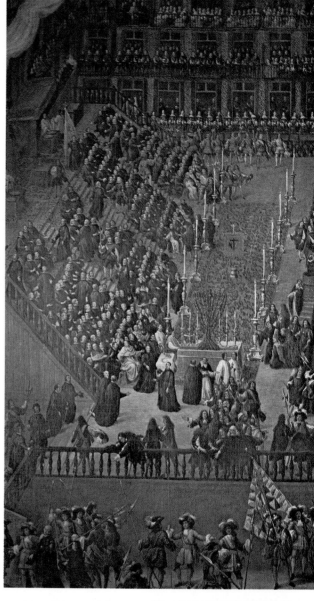

Above, an Inquisition torture room in Würtemberg, an ecclesiastical principality in Germany. The auto-da-fé (near right) was a public ceremony in which those tried by the Inquisition appeared in robes and hoods to hear their sentences. This painting shows an auto-da-fé in Madrid in 1680.

In 1478, King Ferdinand and Queen Isabella asked Pope Sixtus IV to establish in Spain a Holy Office of the Inquisition to aid in enforcing religious orthodoxy and in reforming abuses among the clergy. The Inquisition became Spain's first truly national institution and a vital instrument in the growth of royal power in that nation.

The principal target of the Spanish Inquisition was never Protestantism, which had virtually no organized strength in Spain, but the *conversos* (converted Jews) and, later, the Morisco minority. Although—or perhaps because—many of the country's most distinguished families had Jewish or Moslem ancestors, there was great popular support for statutes of *limpieza de sangre,* which required candidates for ecclesiastical and secular offices to prove that they came from pure-blooded Christian backgrounds. Racial and ethnic prejudices were thus combined with the persecution of religious nonconformism.

The use of secret informants and the practice of confiscating the property of the accused generated a climate of fear throughout Spain. Even Archbishop Bartolomé de Carranza, who had once been Mary Tudor's confessor, was imprisoned for seventeen years on undisclosed charges.

Above, Tomás de Torquemada, the first inquisitor general of Spain. Left, Cardinal Francisco Jiménes de Cisneros, inquisitor general of Castile and León (in northwest Spain) after 1507. He is leading an expedition to North Africa.

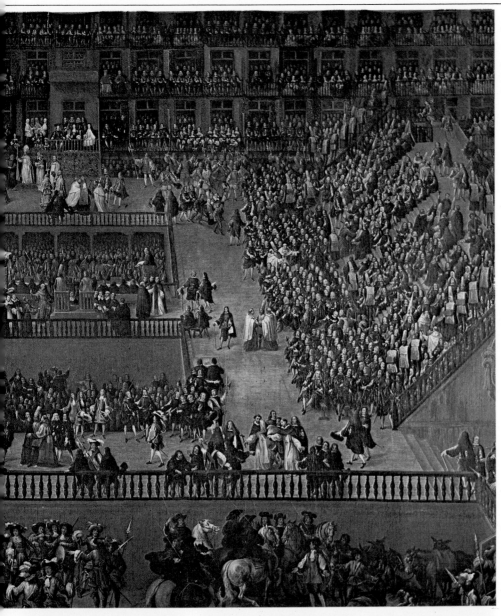

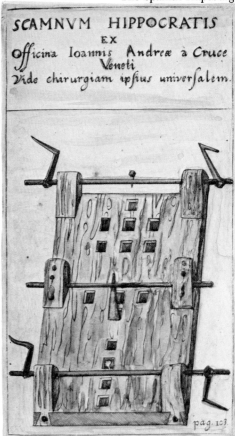

SCAMNVM HIPPOCRATIS
EX
Officina Ioannis Andreæ à Cruce
Veneti
Vide chirurgiam ipsius universalem.

pag. 103

Instruments of torture employed by the Inquisition included the rack (above) and the so-called waker (below), in which weights were hung from the accused to prevent him from falling asleep. The use of torture to extract confessions was common throughout Europe at the time.

Ignatius Loyola (above), the founder of the Jesuits, was interrogated by the Inquisition in 1526 and forbidden to preach for three years. Near right, another portrait of Cardinal Jiménes, who reformed many abuses in the Spanish church while increasing the powers of the Holy Office.

Left, Philip III as a youth. Above, the duke of Lerma, Spanish prime minister under Philip, in a painting by Rubens.

Hapsburg Europe, meanwhile, was rife with plots to assassinate Elizabeth and replace her with Mary Stuart. Don John of Austria, the illegitimate son of Charles V and the hero of Lepanto, schemed to launch a lightning raid from the Netherlands and establish himself as king at Mary's side. Bernardino de Mendoza, a Spanish ambassador, conducted a secret correspondence with Mary, in the course of which she agreed to make Philip her heir in place of her heretic son, James of Scotland. The discovery of Mendoza's involvement in an assassination plot led by the English Catholic dandy Anthony Babington finally sealed Mary's fate. In February 1586, Elizabeth signed her rival's death warrant.

Philip was quick to express outrage at Mary's execution and now was more inclined than ever to approve of the full-scale invasion that had been urged on him since 1585. With Mary dead, England's throne would be his to dispose of as he wished once Elizabeth was eliminated. When he finally conquered his indecision, though, Philip found that there were substantial practical problems to overcome. Santa Cruz, Spain's greatest admiral, estimated that the enterprise would require five hundred ships, outfitted and manned at a cost of more than four million ducats. The sum was appalling even to a free-spending Hapsburg, and at length a compromise plan was adopted. A much smaller fleet was to sail from Lisbon, rendezvousing in the Netherlands with the army of Alessandro Farnese; Farnese's army would then cross the English Channel on barges under the fleet's escort.

The scheme inspired nothing but misgivings in those who were assigned to carry it out. Santa Cruz dragged out the preparations for sailing, stalling for time and money to remedy the inadequacies of his fleet. An unanticipated delay was brought on in 1587, when Sir Francis Drake led an English raid on the port of Cádiz and destroyed a large supply of barrel staves, which were essential to provisioning the Span-

Near left, a Rubens painting of Philip III's younger son, the cardinal-infante Ferdinand, shortly after he led the Catholic armies to a victory over the Swedes at Nördlingen in 1634. Appointed a cardinal-archbishop at the age of ten, Ferdinand was a dashing figure who much preferred the battlefield to the church. Far left, a courtyard in the College of Saint Gregorio, located in the city of Valladolid. The elaborately detailed gallery is characteristic of the Spanish plateresque style, so called because it is reminiscent of ornamental plata, *the Spanish word for silver.*

ish Armada's ships. Spanish misfortunes reached their peak when Santa Cruz died a week before the Armada was due to sail.

To succeed this experienced sailor Philip chose the duke of Medina-Sidonia, a man who had never been in command during an engagement at sea. Aghast, the duke begged to be excused, noting in a letter to the king's secretary: "I know by experience of the little I have been to sea that I am always seasick and always catch cold." Such honesty did not, however, induce Philip to reconsider the appointment.

No doubt Medina-Sidonia would have been even more despairing had he realized that the key point of

the plan, the rendezvous with Farnese, would never take place. (Farnese had repeatedly warned that a Dutch boycott could prevent his barges from ever leaving port. Since the Spanish galleons were incapable of maneuvering in shallow water, there would be nothing that could be done militarily to prevent this.) Bound by orders that doomed his mission to failure, Medina-Sidonia set sail with the Armada on May 9, 1588.

Although the Armada was reputed to be invincible, the commanders and crew could not have been more gloomy. As one of the captains acknowledged at his departure: "We are sailing in the confident hope of a miracle." The Armada's first encounter with the English went far better than expected, but the "miracles," when they occurred, all worked to the benefit of the English. Having been dispersed by English fire ships, the fleet was driven by a fierce gale into the North Sea. Storms pursued the Spanish ships around the northern tip of Scotland, and as the Armada limped southward nearly half of the remaining vessels

Below, a Rubens portrait of Philip IV as a young man. Rubens visited Spain twice and received numerous commissions from the Spanish Hapsburgs. Below right, coins issued during Philip IV's reign, depicting the king's second wife, Mariana de Austria, and the king himself.

were wrecked against the rocky coasts of Scotland and Ireland.

At the time, few realized that Spain's ambitious foreign policy had foundered along with its Armada. Philip, on hearing that his invasion of England had failed, merely remarked: "I sent my ships against men, not against the winds and storms"; he then set about planning a second strike. As war with England dragged on for more than a decade, though, Philip grew increasingly pessimistic about the prospects for success.

During this period, Philip became ever more pre-occupied with the civil war in France, which pitted the Protestant Huguenots against the ultra-Catholic Guise party. The assassination of the duke of Guise with the complicity of Henry III and the murder of the king himself a few months later created what seemed a perfect opportunity to advance the claims of Isabella, Philip's daughter by Elizabeth of Valois. The Spanish ambassador proposed to the ultra-Catholic leadership of France that Isabella, married to a suitable French prince, would make a desirable alternative to the Huguenot heir of Henry III, Henry of Navarre.

This daring scheme might have succeeded had not the Spanish diplomats been carried away by their own arrogance. They wanted to reserve to themselves the right to choose Isabella's bridegroom and even hinted that Albert of Austria might be preferable to any French candidate. While negotiations languished, Henry of Navarre rendered the whole question moot by deciding in 1593 that Paris was "worth a mass." Henry embraced Catholicism, France accepted Henry, and Philip was faced with a unified, hostile France.

The chronic economic problems that plagued the Hapsburgs came to the fore several years later, in 1596, when Philip was forced—for the third time during his reign—to declare bankruptcy. In an era when European monarchs were fighting for the right to impose regular taxes on their subjects, Philip was by no means alone in having financial difficulties. The

Although Philip II moved his court to Madrid in 1560, Toledo remained the ecclesiastical capital of Spain. As one of Toledo's admirers wrote: "Her hour of decadence took on the air of strength, so that the evening seemed to shine more brightly than the noontide." Among the city's best known monuments are its cathedral (left), which was completed in 1493, and the plateresque portal of the Hospital de Santa Cruz (above).

Left, the last of a series of portraits that immortalized the image of the infanta Margaret Theresa, Philip IV's youngest daughter. Margaret Theresa married Leopold of Austria when she was fifteen and died seven years later.

The Maids of Honor *(right) is perhaps Velázquez' most famous work. It depicts Velázquez (at the left of the painting, holding the palette) being interrupted by the five-year-old infanta Margaret Theresa and her maids, including two dwarfs.*

The Spain of Velázquez

Born in 1599 to an affluent Seville family, Diego Rodríguez de Silva y Velázquez arrived in Madrid at the age of twenty-three, just as the count of Olivares, Philip IV's newly appointed prime minister, was attempting to clamp down on extravagant court spending with a series of austerity measures. Although the royal family could no longer afford the brilliant pageantry it had enjoyed under Philip III, retrenchment did not come easily. The depressed economy had made the court a magnet for the families of grandees, eminent nobles who were no longer able to support themselves on their shrinking estates, and for the thousands of lesser nobles and commoners who hoped to earn a living in service to higher aristocrats.

A masterly technician, Velázquez devoted much of his career to painting portraits of the royal family. Subjects like the homely and licentious Philip IV (far left) and his queen, Mariana de Austria (near left), could not have offered Velázquez much inspiration.

Above, Elizabeth of Bourbon, Henry IV's daughter and Philip IV's first wife, in a luxurious gold-embroidered riding costume. Below, the cardinal-infante Ferdinand, the king's younger brother, in hunting gear. Marie Thérèse (this page, bottom left) was Philip IV's daughter by his first wife. Upon her marriage to Louis XIV of France, Marie Thérèse was forced to renounce all claims to the Spanish throne for herself and her descendants. Louis regarded this as a promise made to be broken. This page, bottom center, the six-year-old Prince Baltasar Carlos, a son of Philip IV.

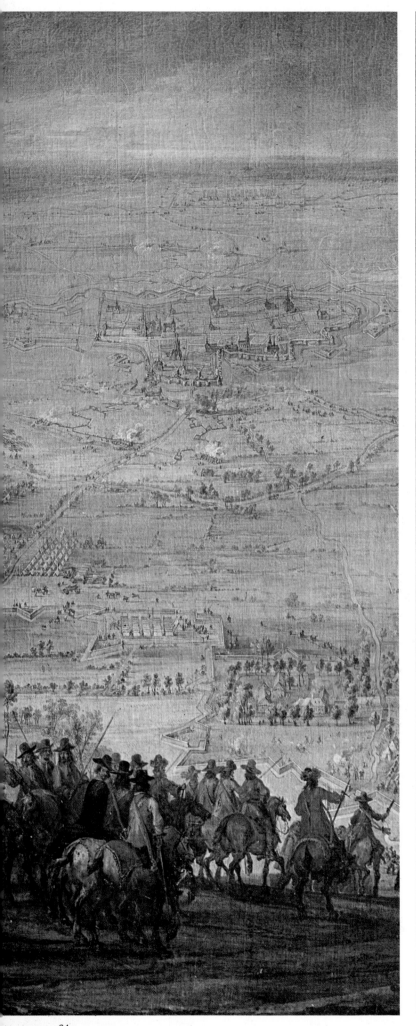

shocking aspect of the situation was that the state of Philip's treasury during the 1590s reflected a collapse of the Castilian economy. Although staggering quantities of silver bullion were still being brought from the mines of the New World, Castile was faced with financial ruin.

The most basic cause of the debacle was that both Charles V and Philip II spent far too much. The lion's share of the Crown's revenues from the New World was never invested in Spain at all but went instead to the Hapsburgs' bankers in Italy and Germany to refinance old loans and to pay for new military adventures. The monarchy was forced to impose heavy taxes on its Castilian subjects—taxes that fell most heavily on farmers and left Castilian agriculture in disarray.

Another, more insidious, problem was inflation. During the sixteenth century, prices in Spain rose four hundred percent, and Castilian manufactured goods became too expensive to compete with foreign-made products. Inept management at the highest levels of government only made matters worse. Castile theoretically had a captive market in its New World possessions, but the Castilian council of finance never formulated a coherent plan to foster industry at home. In fact, the council's regulations and tax policies often had precisely the opposite effect. The most productive element of the Castilian population was subject to the most burdensome taxation, while the nobility, which was generally exempt from taxes, was free to invest its fortunes in ostentatious homes, furniture, and art objects.

In sum, Philip's rule left Castile in worse economic shape than it had been in under his father—worse, in fact, than that of many lesser Hapsburg territories, where it had been politically unfeasible to tax so heavily. Nevertheless, the aged king, as his life drew to a close, was able to convince himself that he was leaving his affairs in good order. In 1598 he made peace with France and appointed Isabella, his daughter, and the archduke Albert, her husband-to-be, rulers of the Netherlands. Having dealt with tem-

Left, a detail of a painting that depicts the siege of Ieper (Ypres), ancient capital of western Flanders, in 1649. Right, seventeenth-century ceramic tiles manufactured by the famous Dutch works at Delft, showing soldiers armed with harquebuses (guns) and pikes (lances).

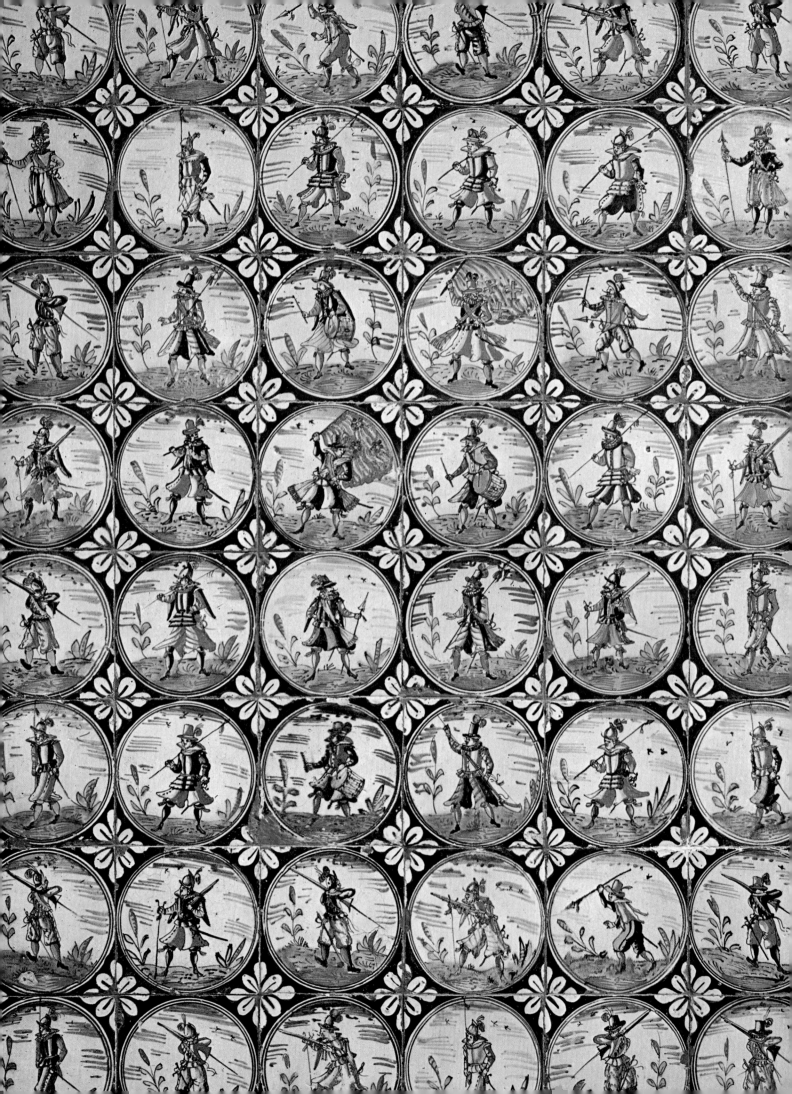

In 1625 the Spanish recaptured the important fortress of Breda in the Netherlands from the Dutch. This famous painting (above) by Velázquez depicts the Dutch governor's surrender.

Below, the count of Olivares as portrayed by Velázquez. Right, the Spanish siege of a stronghold in French Flanders.

poral affairs, Philip spent his last months in the Escorial, the royal residence outside Madrid, surrounded by his spiritual advisers and his vast collection of saints' relics. To the end, throughout an agonizing final illness, Philip's legendary self-control never faltered. He died on September 3, 1598.

At the end of his long life, Philip had expressed only one regret: "That God, who has given me so many kingdoms, has not granted me a son fit to govern them." The sentiment of this statement was all the more poignant because Philip, in four marriages, had fathered no fewer than nine children. Five infants born to his last wife, Anna of Austria, had died. Only two children, his daughters by Elizabeth of Valois, had given him any happiness. Don Carlos, one of his two sons to survive infancy, had caused him no end of misery.

Descended on both sides of his family tree from Juana la Loca, Don Carlos showed signs of abnormality early in his youth, pursuing such "amuse-

ments" as torturing horses. In 1562, at the age of seventeen, Don Carlos fell down a flight of stairs (gossip had it that he was chasing a porter's daughter); after surgery to heal his injuries, the young man became prey to violent fits and paranoid delusions. Convinced that his father was planning to have him killed, Don Carlos secretively made plans to leave the country. Philip, who foresaw that his deranged son might become a dangerous weapon in the hands of Spain's enemies, had his heir placed under arrest. Six months later, in July 1568, Don Carlos died in his prison quarters.

The death was a personal and dynastic tragedy for Philip, and the circumstances surrounding it plunged the king into a storm of controversy. Some said that Don Carlos had been murdered because he was a secret Protestant, others claimed that he was passionately in love with his stepmother, Elizabeth of Valois. Philip's refusal to visit his dying son and later to show his grief in public fanned the rumors that he had indeed killed Don Carlos.

The second of Philip's sons who survived to manhood succeeded to the throne as Philip III in 1598. Philip III inherited his father's red hair and slight physique and his grandfather's Hapsburg jaw. He departed entirely from the example of his progenitors, however, in that he was absolutely indifferent to affairs of state. He fulfilled his duty as king by marrying Margaret of Austria, his cousin, and fathering eight children. All other business he preferred to delegate to his favorite adviser, Francisco Sandoval y Rojas, the duke of Lerma. The son of a king who had prided himself on his attention to the smallest details of government business, Philip was wont to exclude official visitors from his court for months at a time. "Their majesties have come here to enjoy themselves and not to deal with business," he would plead.

The powerful duke of Lerma undertook to pursue a policy of peace. After a disastrous attempt to make common cause with the Irish rebels Tyrone and O'Donnell, he concluded a treaty in 1604 with James I of England, Elizabeth's successor. He negotiated a

Top, Dutch ships attacking the Spanish at the battle of The Downs, fought in a neutral roadstead in the English Channel in 1639. Admiral Maarten Tromp (immediately above) commanded the Dutch fleet, which succeeded in capturing or destroying forty-three of the fifty-one Spanish vessels. Right, the governor of Cádiz (shown seated) giving orders for the defense of his city. The English siege of this Spanish port in 1625 was prompted by a dispute over Spain's occupation of the Palatinate (in western Germany), whose elector was related to the Stuart family of England and Scotland by marriage. This painting—by Francisco de Zurbarán, an eminent representative of the Spanish Baroque—was displayed as a companion piece to Velázquez' depiction of the surrender of Breda.

twelve-year truce with the United Provinces of the Netherlands and disposed of the nagging question of the Moriscos by ordering the expulsion of more than 110,000 Morisco men, women, and children from Spain. This last act, while hardly humanitarian, was at least less harsh than some alternatives proposed at the time.

Lerma's ascendance at court set an unfortunate pattern for the rule by *validos,* or royal favorites, each of whom enriched his family, his friends, and his friends' families at the expense of the state. Lerma himself squandered unprecedented sums on court festivities, royal weddings, balls, masques, and reli-

gious pageants. During his rule, Spain issued for the first time a *vellón* (debased silver) currency, a measure that even the free-spending Philip II had avoided. Spanish doubloons and pieces of eight, famed throughout the world, soon became so scarce at home that by 1624 churchmen were complaining that they could not purchase copies of papal bulls because payment in silver was required and there was no unde-based silver money to be had.

By Philip III's time, the flow of newly mined silver from the New World's mines had slowed dramatically. The colonies were turning to agriculture, investing their capital at home, and developing their own industries. In Spain, on the other hand, the spirit that had once fostered the growth of industry was all but dead. Rampant inflation, onerous taxes, and social sanctions against manual labor and commercial activity all discouraged would-be entrepreneurs. The surfeit of nobles also had a deleterious effect on eco-nomic development. In some villages, everyone was an *hidalgo,* or member of the lowest-ranking nobility. These hidalgos often had only a very small income from land rents—and sometimes no income at all—yet they disdained active work except for the traditional service to the state and the Church. Conditions varied from province to province and from individual to individual, but too often, they proved the truth of Cervantes' portrait of the hidalguía—a class addicted to genteel impoverishment, clinging to anachronistic chivalric values.

This age of *desengano,* or political disengagement, was a brilliant one for literature and the arts. The

Spain of the poor

By the seventeenth century, Spain had become a country in which ostentatious wealth existed side by side with demoralizing poverty. The collapse of the urban economy had destroyed any semblance of a middle class, and unemployment ran scandalously high. Overwhelmed by the burdens of taxation and debt, peasants deserted the land to live in crowded and filthy towns. The sons of the lesser nobility competed for places in the Church and the bureaucracy, the only institutions where they could hope to earn an honorable living. The freedom of women, meanwhile, was greatly restricted by rigid customs that reflected Spain's contacts with Moorish culture.

Although the plight of the majority of the people was grim, genre paintings by Velázquez, Bartolomé Esteban Murillo, and other masters captured the mood of vitality and exuberance that survived in spite of material poverty. Murillo, who never received the patronage of the court, produced many scenes of lower-class life in southern Spain, including realistic works on such humble themes as a grandmother delousing a child.

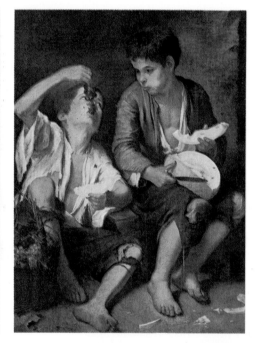

Above, two paintings by Murillo, showing street urchins counting money (left) and enjoying a repast of grapes and melons (right). The combination of genre themes and dramatic lighting, inspired by the Italian painter Michelangelo da Caravaggio, was appreciated by the same wealthy patrons who enjoyed picaresque literature.

The Spinners (right) by Velázquez interprets the mythological theme of the spinning contest between Arachne and Athena in terms of seventeenth-century reality. The foreground figures were probably based on weavers in the royal tapestry works of Madrid.

The young Velázquez painted numerous works of the type known as bodegones—a Spanish term, literally meaning "chophouse" or "winehouse," that came to refer to interior genre scenes and still-life paintings depicting food. The Old Cook (left) is typical of the unsentimental realism of the bodegones. The dignified treatment accorded such down-to-earth scenes was a matter of controversy with later critics; one eighteenth-century writer attributed work of this sort to the artist's desire "to be first in coarseness rather than second in delicacy." Above, The Water Carrier, also by Velázquez.

Murillo depicted the Biblical meeting between Rebecca and Eleazar (near right) as though it had occurred at a town well in Spain. Far right, Laughing Girl with Tambourine, a painting by José de Ribera.

golden age of Castilian literature might be said to have begun some sixty years before Philip III—in 1536, when Charles V chose to speak Castilian during an audience at the Vatican, thus elevating the language to international status. Castilian served as the language of the great narratives of New World exploration and conquest. By the mid-sixteenth century, poets like Garcilaso de la Vega and novelists like the anonymous author of the picaresque adventure *Lazarillo de Tormes* had produced the first masterpieces in Castilian. After the antiforeign decrees of the Inquisition in 1599, Spain gradually grew more removed from the mainstream of European intellectual life.

The early seventeenth century—when Miguel de Cervantes Saavedra wrote his celebrated *Don Quixote*—saw, however, a brilliant flowering of Spanish drama, with the plots of Lope de Vega and Tirso de Molina widely imitated throughout Europe. The polished, elegant works of Pedro Calderón de la Barca, the last of the dramatists of this golden age, best expressed the theme that was coming to dominate Spain's literary consciousness: the transitory nature of human happiness and the eternal beauty of the soul.

After the death of Philip III in 1621, the king's sixteen-year-old son came to the throne as Philip IV.

Preceding pages, a view of the Aragonese city of Saragossa, painted by Velázquez in 1650. Left, an idealized portrait of Charles II, the son of Philip IV, as a child. Juan Carreño de Miranda painted this more realistic likeness (below) when Charles was about twelve years old.

More energetic and intelligent than his father, Philip IV seemed to hold out the hope of an age of national renewal. As one contemporary wrote optimistically of the new king: "His actions promise another Charles V; his words recall his grandfather; his religion reflects his father."

Only the third observation proved accurate. A patron of painters and playwrights, an excellent horseman, and a tireless pursuer of women, Philip's interest in state business—while considerably greater than his father's—was never sufficient to overcome the dominating influence of the royal advisers. Chief among these was Gaspar de Guzmán, the count of Olivares, who became Philip's prime minister.

At the time Olivares took over the reins of government, Spain was still recognized abroad as a great power and the Spanish Hapsburgs were acknowledged to be the senior branch of the imperial family. Even though the signs of decline were there for all to see, the inheritance of Charles V had been preserved virtually intact for almost seventy years—a long time in that turbulent era. Spanish imperialism was feared in Protestant Europe to a degree that bore little relation to its actual strength. That others believed in Spain's power was all to the country's advantage; that Olivares shared the belief proved calamitous.

Left, Louis XIV of France, on horseback, preparing to capture the city of Mons. The fate of this provincial capital of the Hainaut region in present-day Belgium was like that of many cities unlucky enough to become pawns in the struggle between France and Spain. Seized by Spain from Louis of Nassau in 1572, Mons was captured by the French in 1691, regained by Spain in 1697, lost to France in 1701, stormed by Prince Eugene of Savoy in 1709, and captured once again by France in 1746. Above, the escutcheon of a Spanish division during the War of the Spanish Succession.

Churches and shrines

The piety of the Iberian church from the earliest times is reflected in the popular saying that "Spain was Christian before Christ." During the Middle Ages, the shrine of Santiago de Compostela in Galicia (northwestern Spain), said to be the burial place of Saint James the Greater, rivaled the Holy Land as a goal of pilgrimages. Faithful Christians from all over Europe thronged the roads to the shrine in such numbers that they were said to be as numerous as the stars. (The Milky Way was called at the time the Way of Saint James.) Largely through the Cistercians and the Benedictines, who maintained the pilgrimage route, Romanesque and Gothic styles of architecture reached Spain. Later, Renaissance influences were felt because of the Italian connections of the Crown of Aragon and the arrival of the Hapsburg monarchs. Nevertheless, Spanish church architecture always displayed a distinctive character. Moorish elements appear frequently, both in the monumental grill work used to enclose interior chapels and in the ornate plateresque façades.

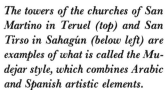

The church of Santo Domingo (left) in Soria has one of the finest Romanesque façades in Spain.

The towers of the churches of San Martino in Teruel (top) and San Tirso in Sahagún (below left) are examples of what is called the Mudejar style, which combines Arabic and Spanish artistic elements.

Above, the twelfth-century church at Santillana del Mar, which stands on the site of one of the earliest Christian churches in Spain. It is said to house the tomb of the fourth-century martyr Saint Juliana. Below, the remains of the Cartuja, a Carthusian monastery that was once among the finest Romanesque buildings in Granada.

Above, a map showing some of the noteworthy churches of Spain and their style of architecture.

The cathedral of Santiago de Compostela is Spain's most celebrated pilgrimage church. The main façade (left) dates from the seventeenth and eighteenth centuries, but the south portal (above) is part of the original twelfth-century structure.

Right, the New Cathedral of Salamanca, a sixteenth-century Spanish Gothic church. The University of Salamanca was long the center of Spain's intellectual life.

Coincidentally, the twelve-year truce between Spain and the United Provinces of Holland expired in the year Philip came to the throne. It was a point of honor with Olivares and Philip IV that the sovereignty of the United Provinces never be recognized, and the decision was made to reopen hostilities in the Netherlands. With this course agreed on, it became essential to secure guarantees for the free movement of Hapsburg armies between the Hapsburgs' Italian possessions and the Low Countries. The need to facilitate passage through the Rhineland inevitably embroiled Spain in the long series of conflicts that came to be known as the Thirty Years' War. Even Spain's most glorious moments in the war seemed to precipitate misfortune. In 1634, for example, when Ferdinand, Philip's younger brother, destroyed the Swedish army at Nördlingen in Bavaria, this evidence of Hapsburg strength so alarmed France that it entered the fray the next year.

With Spain at war once again, it became more necessary than ever to increase the Crown's income. Olivares saw clearly that Castile had been sapped dry through taxation and that his only hope lay in redistributing the tax burden among the various Hapsburg possessions. His plan, called the Union of Arms, was directed especially at Portugal and the ancient Spanish kingdoms of Aragon, Valencia, and Catalonia, whose independent-minded Cortes had long resisted all calls to pay the expenses of a monarchy they considered basically Castilian. Olivares' proposal was in many ways a sensible one, but his timing could hardly have been worse. If the provinces had not been persuaded to join their fortunes to Castile when it was wealthy, why would they have done so when it was impoverished?

By the mid-1630s, Catalonia became the focal point of Olivares' frustrations. Although the war with France was going badly, Catalonia still refused to supply troops, citing an ancient constitutional provision that prevented its Cortes from recruiting soldiers

In the War of the Spanish Succession, Austria, England, and France allied to oppose Philip of Anjou's claim as heir to the territories of the Spanish Hapsburgs. Among the allies' victories were Audenarde (above left), where in 1708 the duke of Marlborough and Eugene of Savoy defeated a combined Franco-Spanish force, and Vigo Bay (left), where in 1702 an Anglo-Dutch fleet bested Spanish galleons brought from the New World under French escort.

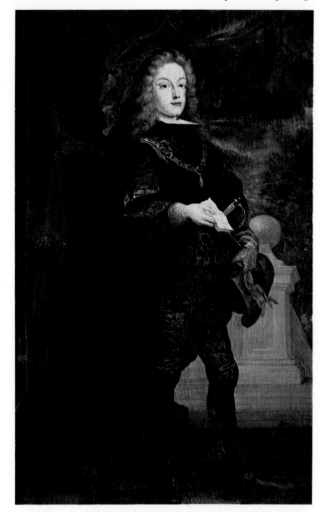

Above, Philip of Anjou, the grandson of Louis XIV. As Philip V, he became the first Bourbon king of France. Charles of Austria (below), Philip's principal rival for the Spanish throne, was elected Holy Roman emperor in 1711.

Gibraltar

Gibraltar's strategic importance as the "key to Spain" was recognized by Queen Isabella in 1502, when she bestowed upon the territory a coat of arms consisting of a castle and a golden key. The rocky promontory, which lies less than ten miles from the Moroccan coast, was fated to be a prime objective during any invasion of Iberia; indeed, it takes its name from the Arabic designation of a mountain honoring Tariq ibn Ziyad, a Moorish leader who captured the Gibraltar peninsula in 711.

Garrisoning a fortress as uninviting as Gibraltar has never been easy. As early as 1311, King Ferdinand IV of Castile proclaimed: "Whoever . . . shall be inhabitants and dwellers therein, whether swindlers, thieves, murderers, or other evildoers whatsoever, or women escaped from their husbands . . . shall be freed or secured from punishment." In the seventeenth century, Charles II hired two Italian engineers to improve Gibraltar's fortifications and build gun placements; the fortress remained, however, undermanned. This weakness was duly noted by English sailors. After more than a century of coveting this strategic outpost, England finally got its chance to conquer Gibraltar during the War of the Spanish Succession. In July 1704, Admiral George Rooke occupied Gibraltar on behalf of the archduke of Austria, England's ally. By terms of the Treaty of Utrecht (1713), the peninsula was ceded to the British government.

Above, a perspective map of Gibraltar's fortifications, executed in Paris during the eighteenth century. The pictures at the bottom of the map show Gibraltar as it appears from the Mediterranean (left) and the Atlantic (right). Left, a view of the Strait of Gibraltar.

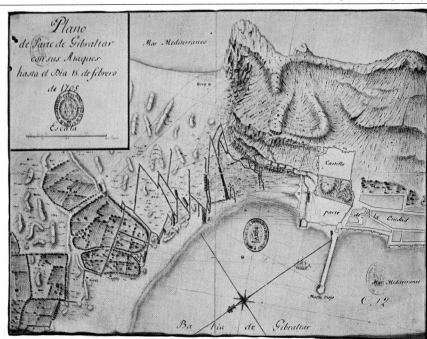

Above, an early eighteenth-century map of Gibraltar. Below, a plan for an attack on Gibraltar drawn up in 1779 by Louis des Balbes de Berton de Crillon, a French duke. France, acting in support of the American colonies, had declared war on Britain, and Spain seized the opportunity to attempt recovery of Gibraltar. The British garrison held out for three years and seven months—surviving the longest continuous siege in history.

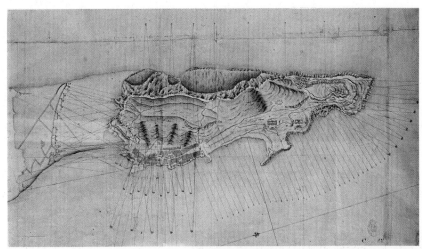

Left, a cannon dating from the seventeenth century, when Gibraltar was in Spanish hands. Right, the remains of a Moorish fortress.

Through their service to the Hapsburgs, rulers of the House of Savoy were able to strengthen their hold over family domains in the Piedmont region of Italy. Right, Emmanuel Philibert. Above, Prince Eugene, a descendant of Emmanuel Philibert.

to fight outside the provinces' borders. Faced with this obstinacy, Olivares decided to bring the front to the Catalans, believing that the shock of war would rally these stubborn provincials to the Crown. He failed to anticipate that the billeting of Spanish troops in the province would be the last straw in what the Catalans regarded as a deliberate policy of neglect and abuse. In May 1640, peasant armies swept through the province, killing Crown servants and native landowners alike. The terrified aristocrats of Barcelona invited the French to occupy their homeland. When French rule proved even more exploitative than Spanish, the Catalans decided, however reluctantly, that there was some advantage to be had in the protection of the Spanish crown. In time, Barcelona was retaken.

Relations between Portugal and Castile too were bitter. Each kingdom had its own overseas empire, a situation that led to constant friction. The Portuguese were convinced that Philip was pursuing his European wars at the expense of defending Brazil; the Castilians, for their part, resented the presence of Portuguese traders and settlers in the Spanish territories of the Río Platte region, Peru, and Mexico. Because many of the Portuguese merchants were converted Jews, Castile had a ready-made excuse to

use the Inquisition as a tool for confiscating their properties; this served to increase tensions. By 1640 the Portuguese nobility decided that it had seen enough of Spanish domination, and one of its number—John, the duke of Braganza—was proclaimed king.

The very next year, the New Spain treasure fleet, crippled by poor maintenance and inept commanders, delayed its sailing until September, well after the beginning of the hurricane season, and was destroyed near Bermuda by a tropical storm; the disaster contributed to the ousting of Olivares in 1643. The expensive foreign wars, however, dragged on. Peace with the Dutch and French did not come until 1648 and 1659, respectively. Even so, desultory attempts to recapture Portugal were not abandoned until 1668. In addition, there were revolts in Naples and Sicily to contend with as well as a brief war against England.

Soon a new problem emerged to threaten the survival of the Spanish Hapsburgs. Rumored to be the father of thirty-two illegitimate children, Philip was having difficulty siring a legitimate heir. His first wife had died, leaving only one surviving daughter, Marie Thérèse. In 1647, Philip contracted a new marriage with Mariana de Austria, his niece. Two years later, Mariana arrived in Madrid, a spirited teenager who

Right, Prince Eugene of Savoy leading the rescue of his family seat of Turin, which had been besieged by French troops. This victory in 1706 brought an end to the Franco-Spanish domination of Italian affairs. The fortified city of Turin, shown in this seventeenth-century map and drawing (below), subsequently became the capital of an independent Piedmontese state.

The battle of Malplaquet (preceding pages), fought in 1709, was the bloodiest engagement of the War of the Spanish Succession, costing the victorious English and Austrian allies some twenty thousand lives. The signing of treaties of Rastatt (above) and Utrecht (right) brought an end to this devastating and costly conflict and solemnized the abandonment of French claims to the Low Countries and Italy.

was appalled to discover that Spanish queens were not even allowed to laugh in public. She had little in common with her forty-two-year-old husband, who spent his nights roaming the streets of his capital in search of debauchery and his days pouring out his guilt in a correspondence with a sympathetic nun.

By this point, the royal family could not even afford the basic necessities of life. Surrounded by ladies in waiting and dressed magnificently, the queen and her stepdaughter sat down to meals that were hardly fit for beggars. On one occasion their dinner consisted of nothing more than a few pieces of chicken, served on crusts of stale bread and swarming with flies. Informed once that the pastry cooks had stopped supplying the royal households because of a large unpaid bill, Mariana removed a valuable ring from her finger and asked a servant to sneak out of the palace and

exchange it for pastries in the market; at this, however, the servant took pity on her and paid for the pastries himself.

In this gloomy atmosphere, Mariana did her best to provide the king with an heir. Her first son, Felipe Próspero, died in infancy, but a second child, Charles, was delivered in 1662 and promptly hailed as an infant "beautiful in features . . . somewhat overplump." It soon became obvious that the optimism of these reports was unfounded. In 1664, when Philip IV died and the heir apparent appeared at a public audience to accept acclamation as Charles II of Spain, sharp-eyed observers noticed that he was unable to stand unaided.

In Charles II the strategic marriages that were the foundation of the Hapsburgs' power were shown to be the family's curse as well. Generations of intermarriage had produced a young man who could never hope to rule in his own right. From the dynastic point of view, the tragedy was not so much that Charles was unfit to rule but that he was Philip IV's only surviving legitimate son. The future of Spain was now dependent on a single individual whose ability to beget an heir was dubious at best.

As he grew to adolescence, Charles was subject to a depressing succession of maladies: fainting spells, digestive upsets, rashes, and suppurating sores. As it turned out, though, the unfortunate king not only survived his first wife, a French princess, but went on to marry a second, the German princess Maria Anna of Bavaria-Neuberg. By 1698, however, Charles' health was deteriorating rapidly, and it became evident that the king was incapable of fathering a child. The wits of the capital summed up the situation in a flippant quatrain:

> Three virgins there are in Madrid:
> The Cardinal's library,
> Medina-Sidonia's sword,
> And the Queen our lady.

Charles eventually began to consider the possibility that the devil might be responsible for his woes. For the remaining years of his life, Charles became the pawn of exorcists, who draped him in relics and

87

magic talismans, terrified him and the queen with their ecstatic trances, and kept the whole court in turmoil over rumors that charms had been buried under the floor of the palace by unknown persons seeking to bewitch the king.

The situation played perfectly into the hands of those who were hoping to influence Charles' choice of a successor. By 1698 the rivalry came down to a two-way competition between the Hapsburg archduke Charles of Austria and Philip of Anjou, the grandson of Louis XIV of France and the Spanish king's half sister. Soon each party was hiring its own exorcists, each hoping to convince the king that the other had cast a spell on him. In the end, Charles' fear of his hard-driving and malicious wife overcame his long-standing dislike of Louis. When a majority of his council of state announced its support for Philip of Anjou—partly because it thought that giving Louis his way insured against partition of the Crown's territories—Charles agreed to follow their advice.

When, on November 1, 1700, the last Spanish Hapsburg died, he thus left all of his lands to his family's traditional enemy, the king of France. Charles' will was bitterly contested—not just by the Austrian branch of the family but also by England and the United Provinces of the Netherlands, both of which feared the increase of French power. The resulting War of the Spanish Succession lasted eleven years and ended with the dismemberment of the Spanish Hapsburg "empire." The Spanish Netherlands (present-day Belgium) and Italy were henceforth dominated by Austria, while Spain was handed over to Philip of Anjou—on the condition that the same individual would never rule both Spain and France. In this protracted war, largely fought outside of the Iberian Peninsula, Spain was more a pawn than a participant. The conflict exacerbated regional tensions, especially between the Catalans, who sympathized with the French, and the Aragonese, who were pro-Austrian. By war's end the autonomous constitutions of both regions had been dissolved, but the spirit of Spanish national unity remained elusive.

In the aftermath of this struggle, Philip of Anjou, now Philip V, applied his slogan of "reform from above" in an attempt to reverse the effects of decades of stagnation. Two centuries of Hapsburg rule, though, had left the country economically depressed and profoundly disillusioned. Like the captive prince in Calderón de la Barca's *Life Is A Dream,* much of Spain seemed convinced that by awakening to reality they could only bring about more violence and squalor. It was easier to take refuge in the enchanted sleep of the soul, where the hopes that had once shone so bright remained forever untarnished.

The Hapsburgs in Central Europe

Seven centuries ago the petty German counts of Hapsburg won a foothold in Austria, the gateway to the ethnically complex but geographically and economically unified basin of the Danube River. Through wars, diplomacy, marriage, and luck, later generations of Hapsburgs were destined to spread their rule northward into Poland, southward deep into present-day Yugoslavia, and eastward to what is now the Soviet Union. Until the mid-seventeenth century, the Hapsburgs were to dream of becoming the supreme rulers of Christendom—and a few leaders of the dynasty almost succeeded in turning these

Preceding page, the Great Gallery in Schön-brunn Palace, Vienna, dating from the mid-eighteenth century. The large fresco on the ceiling glorifies the reign of Maria Theresa.

dreams into tangible power. After 1650, with these ambitions shattered, the Hapsburgs began welding their diverse subjects into a modern bureaucratic empire in the Danubian basin. Ultimately, however, fervent modern nationalism turned the Hapsburgs' empire into a ramshackle anachronism, destined to be swept away at the end of World War One.

Political influence has long been an objective of those who rule in the Danubian basin, not only for exploitation of the area's abundant riches but also as a defense against aggressors, for the region offers invading forces an easy route into the heart of Europe. Although the economic and strategic advantages of

The Hapsburg dynasty ruled over some of the most spectacular lands in Europe. Clockwise from top left: the Arlberg pass in Austria, a Danube landscape, the Danube River, the Inn River, the Lake of Four Corners in Switzerland, and the Lepenskivir area of Yugoslavia.

unity in the Danube were ever present, the region was never destined to emerge as a single political entity; nationalism played too decisive a role in the history of east-central Europe to encourage attempts toward unification. Although most of the east-central Europeans are Slavs—Poles, Czechs, Slovaks, Slovenes, Croats, and Serbs—two other groups have grown up in their midst: The Romanians, who speak a Romance language and claim descent from Roman colonists, and the Magyars, or Hungarians, by origin a Turkic people who invaded Europe in the ninth century. Throughout the centuries the diversity of nationalistic sentiments within the confines of the Danubian basin stood as a formidable barrier to political unity.

East-central Europe's historical geography is both enriched and complicated by the disparate social, political, and cultural traditions of its peoples. At one time or another during the last thousand years, almost every one of these nationalities has enjoyed independence, several have ruled over their weaker neighbors, and all have known the bitter experience of conquest and foreign domination. Since the Middle Ages, the history of east-central Europe has been marked by alternating phases of political integration and disintegration, of the advance of foreign masters and the resurgence of native peoples, of the rise and decline of indigenous elites, and of protracted struggles between governing and subjugated classes and nations.

One of the most tenacious and far-reaching influences in the history of Danubian Europe has been that of the Austrian branch of the Hapsburg dynasty. By the late thirteenth century, the consolidation of the Hapsburgs' rule in the Danubian basin was inseparably intertwined with the decline of the medieval Holy Roman Empire, and between the fifteenth and seventeenth centuries the fate of the Austrian Hapsburgs was closely tied to the other branch of the dynasty that ruled in Spain and the Netherlands.

By the mid-seventeenth century, the Hapsburgs had elected for hereditary rule over Hungary and Bohemia, as well as over Austria. Adopting—sometimes to excess—bureaucratic methods of administration, the Hapsburg Empire in the late seventeenth century emerged as one of the most influential states of modern Europe. In the century after the Congress of Vienna (1814–1815), the empire saw its power gradually eroded and its sway diminished. But up until the final cataclysm of World War One, Hapsburg rulers never completely relinquished their medieval ancestors' aspirations to "universal rule."

Once modern nationalist movements evolved among the east-central European peoples in the early nineteenth century, the Hapsburg multinational state seemed anachronistic, even oppressive. The great nineteenth-century Czech historian and patriot Palacký, recognizing that his people could scarcely hope to survive alone in a world of aggressive great nation states, appealed to the Hapsburgs to transform their empire from one of forced political unity into a genuine federation of smaller nationalities possessing equal rights. "If Austria did not exist, it would be necessary to invent it," he wrote, convinced that these people needed some type of unity for their survival. How the Hapsburgs brought the Austrian Empire into existence, and how it eventually disintegrated in the national and social upheavals of World War One is most intelligently understood in the full context of the evolution of the Hapsburg monarchy in central Europe.

In 1570, Hochosterwitz Castle (left) was constructed in Carinthia, in southern Austria, on such an impregnable mountain peak that it was never besieged. Right, Tarasp Castle, in the Engadine valley, Switzerland. Immediately below, a medieval bridge over the Inn River, Austria. Below right, Fort Geroldseck, in the Austrian town of Kufstein. In 1348, Emperor Charles IV built Karlstein Castle (bottom), in Bohemia, to house the crown jewels.

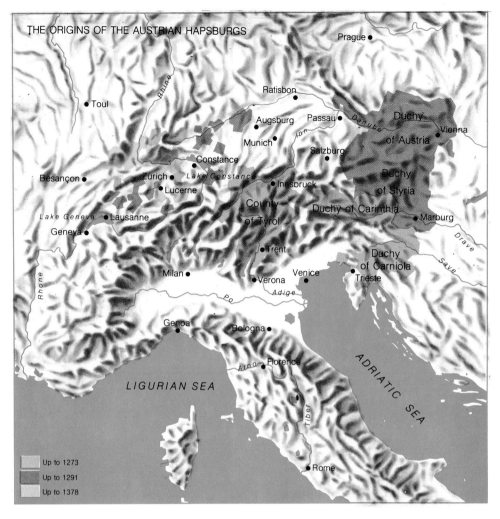

THE ORIGINS OF THE AUSTRIAN HAPSBURGS

Prague
Ratisbon
Toul
Augsburg
Passau
Duchy of Austria
Munich
Vienna
Salzburg
Constance
Besançon
Zurich
Innsbruck
Duchy of Styria
Lucerne
County of Tyrol
Lausanne
Duchy of Carinthia
Marburg
Geneva
Trent
Duchy of Carniola
Milan
Venice
Trieste
Verona
Genoa
Bologna
Florence

LIGURIAN SEA

ADRIATIC SEA

Rome

Up to 1273
Up to 1291
Up to 1378

THE AUSTRIAN HAPSBURGS
IN THE SEVENTEENTH CENTURY

Vistula
Leipzig
Breslau
Dresden
Silesia
Kraków
Prague
Bohemia
Moravia
Metz
Strasbourg
Kahlenberg
Vienna
Munich
Bavaria
Bratislava
Salzburg
Buda
France
Swiss
Innsbruck
Graz
Hungary
Bern
Confederation
Tyrol
Carinthia
Duchy
Carniola
Temesvar
Duchy
Milan
Venice
Karlowitz
Turin
of Milan
Venetian Republic
of Savoy
Belgrade
Danube
Avignon
Po
Nikopol
Nice
Florence
Sarajevo
Marseille
Papal
Sofia
States
Ragusa
Rome
Kingdom
Ottoman Empire
Naples
of Naples
Athens
Corinth
Palermo

MEDITERRANEAN SEA

Dominions of the Hapsburgs at the beginning of the seventeenth century
Territory acquired by the Treaty of Karlowitz (1699)

The Hapsburg domains

In September 1273, the Hapsburg count Rudolf was elected Holy Roman emperor as Rudolf I. His accession marked the beginning of an empire that was destined to encompass much of eastern Europe. By the time of Rudolf's death in 1291, the duchies of Styria and Austria had come under Hapsburg control. By 1379, when Rudolf IV's two brothers partitioned the Hapsburg lands, the dynasty had extended its rule to include the duchies of Carniola and Carinthia as well as the Tyrolean region.

The religious turmoil that permeated Europe in the sixteenth and seventeenth centuries led to the outbreak of the Thirty Years' War between Catholics and Protestants in 1618. The Peace of Westphalia (1648), which ended the war, forced Austria to cede some of its western possessions, thus causing the Hapsburgs to shift their sights eastward. Unfortunately for Austria, the Turkish front, quiet during the Thirty Years' War, once again became active in the 1660s. The Turks engaged the Hapsburgs in a series of wars that for a time posed a direct threat to the Hapsburg capital at Vienna (below, a Turkish insignia captured during the unsuccessful campaign against Vienna in 1683). Stung by a number of decisive setbacks in the late 1680s and 1690s, though, Turkey eventually negotiated the Treaty of Karlowitz (1699), by which all of Turkish Hungary passed to the Hapsburgs.

Renewed conflict with the Turks erupted in the early eighteenth century. Initially victorious, the Hapsburgs acquired a number of Turkish territories by

THE EMPIRE AFTER THE
CONGRESS OF VIENNA (1815)

Poland

Saxony

Prague

Vienna

Bavaria

Munich

Salzburg

Buda

France

Zurich

Graz

Bern

Innsbruck

Switzerland

Bolzano

Trent

Kingdom of

Lombardy-Venetia

Grenoble

Turin

Milan

Venice

Belgrade

Danube

Nikopol

Sardinia

Sarajevo

Avignon

Papal

Sofia

Nice

Genoa

States

Ragusa

Ottoman Empire

Kingdom
of the
Two Sicilies

Kingdom of
Sardinia

Corinth

Athens

MEDITERRANEAN SEA

the Treaty of Passarowitz (1718). Additional gains resulted from an alliance with Great Britain, France, and the Netherlands (the Quadruple Alliance). Losses to the Turks in the middle of the century, however, reduced the Hapsburg domains substantially and, more important, greatly diminished Hapsburg prestige. Austria nonetheless remained a power to be reckoned with. In 1772 it acquired the part of Poland known as Galicia and two years later added an area to the southeast (Bukovina).

Persistent strife plagued the empire from the end of the eighteenth century until 1815, when the Congress of Vienna—the largest peace conference ever held in Europe—concluded. One of the leading figures at the congress was Klemens von Metternich (above), Austria's foreign minister. The congress redrew almost every boundary in Europe, and the Austrian Empire gained control of one and one half times as much territory as it had in 1809.

The Age of Metternich (1815–1848) was fraught with conflict. Emergent forces of nationalism among the many peoples of the empire led to numerous uprisings. The revolutions of 1848 brought about a resurgence of the absolutism that had characterized earlier periods in Hapsburg history. Nationalism, however, was still very much in evidence, and dissension persisted throughout Europe into the twentieth century. Among the repercussions of a conflict between Austria and Serbia in 1909 was the assassination of Archduke Francis Ferdinand in 1914—an event that sparked World War One.

ON THE EVE OF
WORLD WAR ONE

Berlin

Prussia

Vistula

Russia

Saxony

Silesia

Prague

Heidelberg

Danube

Vienna

Paris

Metz

Strasbourg

Bavaria

Budapest

Munich

France

Graz

Bern

Lausanne

Switzerland

Trent

Zagreb

Lyon

Trieste

Fiume

Romania

Turin

Milan

Venice

Belgrade

Danube

Po

Kingdom

Bosnia

Serbia

Marseille

Nice

Sarajevo

Florence

Montenegro

of Italy

Albania

Rome

Macedonia

Naples

Athens

Greece

Palermo

Tunis

MEDITERRANEAN SEA

Bosnia (annexed October 1908)

The origins, both legendary and historical, of the Hapsburg dynasty stretch back to the early years of the medieval Holy Roman Empire in the tenth century A.D. The first Hapsburgs were minor counts from the southwestern German region of Swabia who aligned themselves with the Saxon dynasty—the first ruling house to organize a monarchical state in Germany. In the year 1020 one of the oldest traceable ancestors of the Hapsburg family, Count Radbot, and his brother-in-law, the warlike Bishop Werner of Strasbourg, were permitted by the Saxon king Henry II to build a castle at the confluence of the Aare and Reuss rivers in what is now Switzerland. The name of their castle—"Habichtsburg," or "hawk's castle"—was eventually shortened to "Habsburg" or "Hapsburg." By the end of the eleventh century members of the family were bearing the title "Count of Hapsburg."

Between the eleventh and thirteenth centuries the Hapsburgs' holdings grew steadily in southwestern Germany and in present-day Switzerland and Alsace. Like other noble families of this period, they aug-

mented their wealth and power by playing off emperors against popes. Eventually, however, the Hapsburgs came to be the allies of the last great medieval Holy Roman emperor, Frederick II, of the House of Hohenstaufen, who was willing to make large concessions to the German nobles and territorial princes in return for their support in his attempt to dominate Italy and the papacy.

The turning point in the Hapsburgs' early development came during the "Great Interregnum" that followed the death of Frederick II in 1250. Germany was thrown into disarray as the territorial princes struggled to capture the imperial crown. The prince who emerged as Germany's ruler from what contemporaries called "the dreadful time without an emperor" was Rudolf of Hapsburg, who in 1273 was elected king of Germany. Rudolf was an able, ambitious, and clever man, skilled at hiding a shrewd and ruthless realism behind a façade of affability, thriftiness, and piety.

Rudolf was the pivotal figure in the Hapsburgs'

Left, a detail of the act by which Margaret Maultasch, countess of Tyrol, ceded her lands to Rudolf IV, the Founder, in 1363. Attached to the document are the seals of Margaret and her fourteen feudatories, or lords. The Hapsburgs' annexation of Tyrol provided a link between the eastern and western parts of their domains. Except for a nine-year period when the county came under Napoleon's control, Tyrol remained a Hapsburg possession until the empire finally dissolved in 1918.

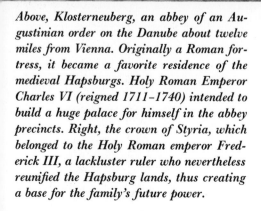

Above left, King Rudolf I, the first Hapsburg to be elected king of Germany, in 1273, from a stained-glass window in St. Stephen's Cathedral, Vienna. Above, the ducal throne, constructed from Roman stones, used by the dukes of Carinthia while receiving oaths of fealty from their subjects. Carinthia was incorporated into the Hapsburg domains by Otto, brother of Duke Albert, the Wise, in 1335.

Above, Klosterneuberg, an abbey of an Augustinian order on the Danube about twelve miles from Vienna. Originally a Roman fortress, it became a favorite residence of the medieval Hapsburgs. Holy Roman Emperor Charles VI (reigned 1711–1740) intended to build a huge palace for himself in the abbey precincts. Right, the crown of Styria, which belonged to the Holy Roman emperor Frederick III, a lackluster ruler who nevertheless reunified the Hapsburg lands, thus creating a base for the family's future power.

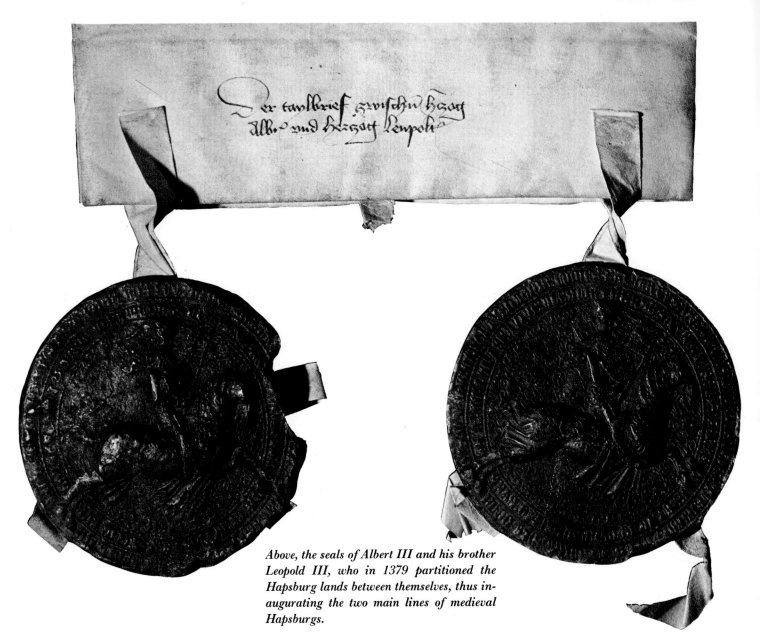

Above, the seals of Albert III and his brother Leopold III, who in 1379 partitioned the Hapsburg lands between themselves, thus inaugurating the two main lines of medieval Hapsburgs.

rise to prominence. As Frederick II's godson, as well as the restorer of royal authority in Germany after the Hohenstaufen dynasty had died out, he stood as the foundation of the Hapsburgs' later claim that they were the only legitimate dynasty of the Holy Roman Empire. Rudolf also successfully established the Hapsburgs in what was eventually to be their homeland: the Danubian basin. By 1278 Rudolf defeated his most formidable rival, the Czech king Ottokar II of Bohemia, seizing Ottokar's provinces of Austria, Styria, Carinthia, and Carniola. Rudolf immediately began to call his dynasty by a new name: the House of Austria.

Rudolf's greatest disappointment was his failure to stem the Holy Roman emperor's loss of political authority. His son Albert, the duke of Austria, was to suffer even greater humiliations. After Rudolf's death in 1291 Albert was passed over by the electors, winning the German crown only by defeating in battle the electors' choice, the ineffectual Rhenish count Adolf of Nassau, in 1298. Albert's resources were crit-

ically weakened by the rebellion of his subjects, both in the Hapsburgs' older homeland in the west and in their more recent Danubian acquisitions. In 1291 the Forest Cantons of Uri, Schwyz, and Unterwalden formed the nucleus of the Swiss Confederation to resist Albert's demands for taxes, while the towns and nobility of Austria forced demeaning concessions on the Hapsburgs, whom they now regarded as foreign intruders.

Lacking his father's talent for inspiring loyalty, Albert was assassinated in 1308 by a nephew who thought he had been cheated of his rightful inheritance. The Hapsburg family thus became embroiled in a debilitating domestic feud, and for more than a century was unable to regain possession of the German crown.

The fourteenth century in Germany—and, indeed, throughout Europe—was an era of protracted economic depression, aggravated by the Black Death of 1348–1349, in which one third of Europe's people are estimated to have perished. As the tax base inevitably

Above, a fifteenth-century portrait of Frederick III, crowned Holy Roman emperor in 1452. By marrying his son Maximilian to Mary of Burgundy in 1477, he achieved a major coup: the extension of the Hapsburgs' territory to encompass Burgundy, the Low Countries (present-day Belgium, the Netherlands, and Luxembourg), and Spain. Frederick III was much disliked by his contemporaries, in part for his egoistic, scheming nature.

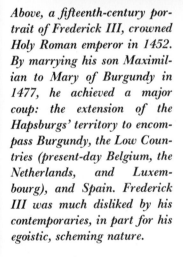

Above left, a portrait of Matthias Corvinus, king of Hungary, who briefly wrested Austria from Hapsburg control in the late fifteenth century. Above, the Schweizer Tor, or Swiss Gate, a Renaissance portal to the Hofburg, a palace built in Vienna in 1552 by Ferdinand, brother of Charles V. Ferdinand's titles are inscribed above the archway. Left, Heinfels Castle, in eastern Tyrol.

shriveled, so did monarchical authority; attempts to arrest the alarming diminution of imperial power only provoked political and social unrest.

The Hapsburgs were no exception to this general pattern of increasing monarchical weakness. A steady decline of revenues from the dynasty's lands and the growing resistance of the local nobility made it impossible for the Hapsburgs to uphold their hitherto sacrosanct principle of collective inheritance. The family's lands had formerly been treated as a unit,

Above left, a statue of Maximilian I, created by Hans Keb in 1491, now at the Klosterneuburg abbey. When residing at his royal lodge (left) at Innsbruck, in Tyrol, the emperor would watch festivities from the balcony. The roof of the lodge produces a goldlike radiance from its shingles, which are made from 3,500 plates of gilded copper. Above, Holy Roman Emperor Maximilian I with his wife and family, in a painting by B. Striguel. The boy in the center, Charles, was to become one of the greatest emperors in history. The rich costumes reflect the luxury of the Burgundian court.

governed by the eldest male but with the income and authority shared among all members; in the fourteenth century, however, pressures to partition the lands among all adult males became overwhelming. Only with the greatest difficulty were the Hapsburg dukes able to retain their position in Germany—and even so, their expansion was confined to their eastern provinces along the Danube. The Hapsburgs' ever-increasing tendency to regard Austria as the primary seat of their power was demonstrated by their choice of traditional Austrian Christian names and their numerous bequests to Austrian monasteries and shrines.

Hapsburg imperial claims were kept alive during the fourteenth century by the energetic and dynamic Count Rudolf IV, the Founder, who was able to achieve much in his seven-year reign (1358–1365). Rudolf married the daughter of Charles IV, the Holy Roman emperor and king of Bohemia, thus reinforcing his own dynasty's claims to the imperial dignity. He meddled openly in the affairs of northern Italy,

This bronze statue (left) depicts Margaret of Austria, the favorite daughter and confidante of Maximilian I. She had a sardonic sense of humor and enjoyed writing poems in French about the fickleness of human fortune. As the guardian of the future Holy Roman emperor Charles V and as regent of the Netherlands, she performed her duties with admirable intelligence, wit, and skill.

Below left, the marriage of Maximilian and Mary of Burgundy commemorated in a brooch decorated with enamel, pearls, and gems. Although Maximilian I was interred in the town of his birth, Wiener Neustadt, his tomb (below) lies in the royal chapel in the Hofkirche at Innsbruck. The sarcophagus, or stone coffin, is surrounded by bronze statues of his relatives.

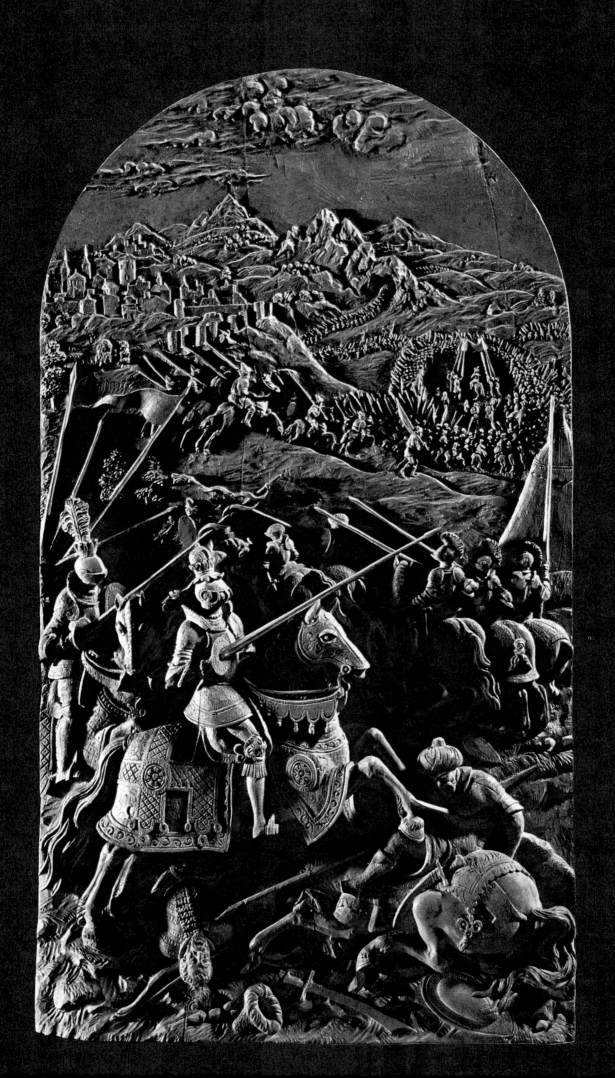

Left, Holy Roman Emperor Charles V in battle, shown in a sixteenth-century carved wooden panel. Charles ruled over a great number of territories, including the hereditary Hapsburg lands, the Holy Roman Empire, Burgundy, Spain, parts of Italy, and the New World. Much of his reign was spent in defending Christendom from the incursions of the infidel Turks and in keeping his own subjects under control.

Above, one of Charles V's administrators supervising preparations for a crusade against Tunis, in North Africa, as depicted in a sixteenth-century Flemish tapestry. Charles can be seen on horseback. A statue of Margaret of Austria (right), regent of the Netherlands in the early sixteenth century, still decorates the front of the Hôtel de Ville at Malines, Belgium.

won some territory near the head of the Adriatic Sea, and in 1363 completed the Hapsburgs' annexation of the mineral-rich province of Tyrol—a convenient link between the family's eastern and western possessions. He also took the first steps to create an administrative structure capable of welding his lands into a single political unit.

Rudolf was a brilliant propagandist. The Hapsburgs already had begun to glory in improbable legends of their descent from Roman patricians and even the Trojans. Chagrined by the emperor Charles IV's exclusion of the Hapsburgs from the ranks of those German princes entitled to elect the Holy Roman emperor, Rudolf retaliated by forging claims to such titles as "Archduke of Austria," "Duke of the Palatinate," "Duke of Swabia," and "Grand Master of the Hunt." The House of Hapsburg, Rudolf asserted, was the highest-ranking family in Germany and the only one truly entitled to the imperial crown.

Rudolf IV's autocratic claims provoked an inevitable reaction after his death in 1365. Ignoring his desire to uphold the principle of primogeniture (the right of the eldest son to inherit all family property), the other Hapsburgs partitioned the dynasty's lands into three sections—a decision applauded by the provincial nobilities and towns alarmed by Rudolf IV's attempts at centralization. Partly because of their perpetual rivalries, the Hapsburgs lost control of their Swiss possessions in a bitter struggle against the alpine peasantry and by 1415 were completely ousted from the region.

At the end of the fourteenth century the Ottoman Turks broke into the Balkan Peninsula and pushed with seemingly irresistible force toward the Danubian basin. Unity around the standard of a powerful dynasty was obviously the only way the east-central European kingdoms could defend themselves against this unexpected threat. Two dynasties at first offered their services as the Danubian region's protectors— the Luxemburgers, heirs of Charles IV, who ruled Bohemia and Hungary, and the Jagellonians, who had recently united the crowns of Poland and Lithuania. The Hapsburgs, the third possible leaders of the resistance, were too weak and divided to take advantage of the situation for the moment. The Luxemburgers' male line, however, ended with the death of Holy Roman Emperor Sigismund in 1437, giving Sigismund's son-in-law, Duke Albert V of Austria, the opportunity to reassert Hapsburg ambitions. Albert not only was elected king of Germany but also managed to persuade the nobles of Bohemia and Hungary to choose him as their monarch—albeit one lacking almost all effective power.

Left, a detail of a portrait of Maximilian II, son of Charles V's brother Ferdinand. Above, Maria of Austria, daughter of Charles V and wife of her cousin Maximilian II.

This sixteenth-century symbolic print (immediately above) depicts a gathering of the major leaders of the Protestant Reformation, even though many of them lived at different times. Luther (with opened book) and Calvin, who established the most influential Protestant movements, are in the middle.

Facing page, above, a portrait of Pope Paul III Farnese, one of the leading figures of the Roman Catholic Counter Reformation in the sixteenth century. Right, a fresco (1588–1589) showing the fathers of the Church assembled in an amphitheater at the Council of Trent.

Albert's reign proved to be short and disastrous, ending with his unexpected death in 1439. With the Turks looming ever more menacingly to the south, no one was willing to trust to luck and hope that Albert's pregnant widow would bear a male child. The Hungarians accordingly elected a member of the Jagellonian family as their next king, and in Bohemia a regency was established under the leadership of one of the great nobles. Among the Austrian Hapsburgs, primacy passed to Albert's rather distant relative, Frederick III of Styria, who was elected king of Germany and in 1452 crowned Holy Roman emperor by the pope.

During Frederick III's long and troubled reign the medieval Holy Roman Empire reached the nadir of its political effectiveness and esteem, and the Hapsburgs slowly groped toward a new foundation for their greatness. Weak, timid, and lazy, Frederick did almost nothing to oppose the arrogant power of his mightiest subjects who, like the higher nobility throughout east-central Europe, openly aimed at making monarchs virtual puppets. In 1474 he made a final renunciation of the Hapsburgs' Swiss territories, and between 1485 and 1491 he was forced to surrender Austria itself to the energetic king of Hungary, Matthias Corvinus.

As the other Hapsburg lines died out, however,

Frederick began to gather the dynasty's lands together. His son Maximilian married the heiress of the duke of Burgundy, Mary, in 1477—a union that promised to unite the Hapsburgs' Austrian lands with the great Burgundian inheritance, a patchwork of provinces in present-day Belgium, the Netherlands, Luxembourg, and northeastern France. In 1490 the last collateral Hapsburg, Sigismund of Tyrol, abdicated in Maximilian's favor, assuring Maximilian a rich source of income necessary for winning election as Holy Roman emperor. Meanwhile Frederick confirmed his dynasty's sole right to the title "archduke," and everywhere he employed the letters AEIOU to symbolize his faith that *Austriae est imperare orbi universo* ("it is Austria's destiny to rule the whole world").

Signs of a more hopeful future became increasingly evident during Frederick's last years. An economic revival spread throughout Europe, stimulating renewed silver production in the Tyrolean mines. The late fifteenth century also saw the dawn of the Renaissance in Germany. Vienna and Innsbruck became centers of humanist learning and artistic patronage; Frederick spent what little money he could raise on building the kernel of the great art collection to which his successors added innumerable masterpieces.

Maximilian I, who became Holy Roman emperor and head of the House of Hapsburg in 1493, was a Renaissance prince—a patron of artists, musicians, and men of letters; a would-be knight errant; a huntsman and mountaineer; and a political schemer. He brought to the previously staid Hapsburg court the full splendor and pompous ritual of the Burgun-

Preceding pages, a panoramic scene depicting Imperial Ambassador Baron Johan Ludwig Kufstein's departure from Constantinople in 1628. His mission was to prevent the Turks from intervening in German affairs. Above, Count Adolf Schwarzenberg, who recaptured the city-fortress of Györ, in Hungary, from the Turks in 1594. Left, an extract of a letter from Louis II, king of Bohemia and Hungary, asking his brother-in-law, Ferdinand of Austria, for help against the Turks. Although Ferdinand cooperated, Louis was killed and his army destroyed at the battle of Mohács in 1526.

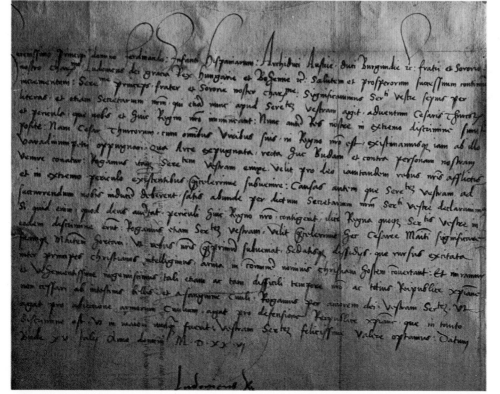

Suleiman the Magnificent (above right), a cultured, learned man and a great warrior, brought the Ottoman Empire to the peak of its power and prestige in the sixteenth century. He besieged Vienna in 1529 and often allied himself with Francis I, king of France, much to the consternation of Europe's Christian rulers. Right, a view of the Danube, seen from the Lepenskivir region of Yugoslavia. The river was the Turks' main route into Austria, and the Danube basin became a major strategic prize in the Hapsburg-Ottoman conflict.

dian dukes. Yet for all his flamboyance and ambition, Maximilian was thwarted in his efforts to strengthen the government of his Austrian possessions. Although he was keenly aware of the need for administrative centralization, extravagance and a perpetual shortage of money prevented him from overcoming the opposition of the tightfisted burghers and nobles who dominated Austria's provincial diets, or local governing assemblies. On at least one occasion the city of Innsbruck refused to open its gates to him because of his failure to pay his debts.

Maximilian made his most important contribution to the rise of the Hapsburgs' empire in the Danubian basin when he concluded a set of dynastic compacts with the Jagellonian king of Poland, Sigismund I, in 1515. Under these treaties Maximilian's grandson Ferdinand married Anne, the sister of the young Jagellonian king Louis II, of Bohemia and Hungary, and Louis in turn married Maximilian's granddaughter Mary. It was stipulated that the dynasty—either Hapsburg or Jagellonian—that first failed to provide a male heir for the crowns of Bohemia, Hungary, or Austria would cede its claims to the other.

The dynastic plans so carefully arranged by Frederick III and Maximilian I came to fruition between 1516 and 1519. Maximilian's eldest grandson, Charles of Ghent, succeeded first to the crowns of

Burgundy, Castile, and Aragon and then, after the older Hapsburg's death, to that of Austria. In 1519, with a prodigious outlay of bribes and other electioneering funds (raised by mortgaging the Tyrolean mines to the wealthy Fugger family), the young man was elected Holy Roman Emperor Charles V. The Hapsburgs stood at the pinnacle of their glory: their goal of becoming the supreme rulers of Christendom seemed a prize within reach.

Charles V was a noble and ultimately tragic figure. Educated in Burgundy by humanist tutors, Charles conscientiously strove to maintain the dignity of his high calling. Aware of the corruption into which the Church had fallen and always holding himself to be at least the pope's equal, Charles resisted the developing Protestant Reformation as a revolt against traditional authority constituted by God, while at the same time sincerely seeking grounds for compromise with the Protestants. He realized that he could not govern his vast but scattered dominions without winning the cooperation of local notables; yet he would tolerate no interference with his plans from the wily French king Francis I or from the German Protestant princes who stubbornly insisted on their autonomy and religious convictions. It was his openly avowed aim to achieve what no medieval Holy Roman em-

peror had ever gained: universal acknowledgment as head of Christendom. Unfortunately for Charles, ineradicable religious dissent, provincial jealousies, and the inevitable shortage of money were destined to stand in his way.

It is ironic that Charles V—who represented to successive generations the epitome of Hapsburg rule—was probably the least Austrian of all the Hapsburgs. French was his native language, and as he grew older he identified more and more with Spain, spoke German only haltingly, and never felt at home in Austria—which, indeed, he scarcely ever visited. Soon after his coronation, Charles decided to make his brother Ferdinand—who was married to the sister of the king of Bohemia and Hungary—not only his representative in Germany but also the ruler of the Hapsburgs' lands along the Danube. With the Turkish threat to east-central Europe becoming greater than ever, Ferdinand needed this secure territorial base around the Danube to defend Germany. Reluctantly Charles also agreed to support Ferdinand's election as his successor to the German crown. In return Ferdinand renounced his claims to Charles' Burgundian patrimony, or inheritance, and to the thrones of Castile and Aragon. Thus the vast Haps-

Above, a relief depicting Elector Palatine Frederick V's flight into exile following the defeat of the Bohemian rebels at the Battle of the White Mountain in 1620. The Winter King, as he was called, ruled Bohemia for only a year. Left, a detail of a stained-glass panel depicting Rudolf II, who became Holy Roman emperor in 1576. Below, an imperial crown surrounded by crown jewels, made by Jan Vermeyen in 1602.

burg realms were divided in two: Charles' descend-ants, ruling Spain and the Netherlands, were to be known as the Spanish Hapsburgs; and Ferdinand's heirs—for whom the Danubian lands and the Holy Roman emperorship were destined—were to become the Austrian Hapsburgs.

The Hapsburgs' consolidation of the other Danu-bian kingdoms with Austria began soon after Charles V invested Ferdinand with his new lands. In 1526 the Turkish sultan Suleiman the Magnificent sent his huge army into Hungary after being refused the trib-ute he had demanded from the Bohemian and Hun-garian king Louis II. Without waiting for reinforce-ments, the frivolous young king engaged the Turks at Mohács and suffered a ruinous defeat. Louis perished without having produced any children, and in ac-cordance with the dynastic arrangements made by Maximilian I in 1515, Ferdinand, Louis' brother-in-law, stood to inherit the deceased ruler's claims in Hungary and Bohemia.

Since both crowns were elective, Ferdinand could succeed Louis only with the consent of the powerful native aristocracies, who were mindful of their rights. In Bohemia the diet duly elected Ferdinand after re-ceiving his solemn pledge to safeguard the country's laws. In Hungary, however, Ferdinand was elected king by one faction of the nobility, and he was able to gain control of only a narrow strip of the country adjoining Austria, as well as the mountains of north-ern Hungary (present-day Slovakia). His rival John

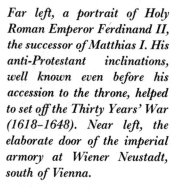

Far left, a portrait of Holy Roman Emperor Ferdinand II, the successor of Matthias I. His anti-Protestant inclinations, well known even before his accession to the throne, helped to set off the Thirty Years' War (1618–1648). Near left, the elaborate door of the imperial armory at Wiener Neustadt, south of Vienna.

Left, a portrait of Maria Anna of Bavaria, Ferdinand II's first wife, painted by Joseph Heintz in 1604. Above right, a detail of a portrait of the emperor's second wife, Eleanor Gonzaga. Following pages, Field Marshall and professional soldier Octavio Piccolomini, with his troops, painted by P. Snayers in 1641.

Zápolya, backed by the Turkish sultan, held Transylvania, Hungary's easternmost province. The Turkish and Hapsburg armies continually fought over control of central Hungary, producing horrible devastation. In 1540 the sultan annexed the region outright, installing a pasha, or Turkish governor, in the Hungarian capital of Buda. In effect, Ferdinand had gained only the prospect of ceaseless wars with the Turks; and Vienna, which was repeatedly besieged, found itself a frontline fortress.

It soon became apparent that Turkish assaults on the Austrian capital were doomed to failure. For each campaign, the Turkish army had to assemble in the spring near Constantinople, then march across the Balkans and along the Danube before engaging the Hapsburg forces. By this time it was invariably autumn and, with the aid of muddy roads and the onset of winter, Ferdinand was able to stave off the Turks, forcing them to retreat. Perceiving this pattern, the Austrian and Bohemian diets and the German princes were exceedingly stingy in providing Ferdi-

Albrecht von Wallenstein

Of all the soldiers of fortune who fought for the Hapsburgs during the Thirty Years' War, none experienced such a meteoric rise to power as Albrecht von Wallenstein. Born in 1583 to a Protestant Bohemian family, he converted to Roman Catholicism in 1606. Following his conversion, Wallenstein entered Ferdinand II's service and made a fortune buying lands confiscated from the Bohemian rebels. By 1623 he owned about a quarter of Bohemia.

Spurred on by ambition, Wallenstein raised an army of twenty thousand fighting men at his own expense, which he controlled for Ferdinand. Commander in chief of the imperial army from 1625, Wallenstein achieved many impressive victories over Europe's Protestant leaders and extended Hapsburg power to the Baltic. But by 1634 his arrogance had become insufferable and Ferdinand ordered his arrest. Before the order was carried out, however, Wallenstein was assassinated by his own officers.

Above, Wallenstein's study at Eger, in present-day Czechoslovakia. Imperial officers commanding Scottish, English, and Irish troops assassinated their general here, outraged at his overbearing manner and insatiable ambition. By 1633 Wallenstein had begun to demand exclusive oaths of loyalty from his officers in the manner of an independent prince. In retaliation, his officers killed him when he was ill and close to military defeat.

Below, a print showing Wallenstein's assassination. He was taken by surprise while asleep and murdered in his nightdress. Ferdinand II was delighted when he heard the news, for he had already instructed Wallenstein's principal lieutenant, Octavio Piccolomini, to capture him dead or alive. Wallenstein did not receive the usual military-style burial; instead his body was thrown onto a heap of corpses collected in a nearby castle.

nand with money to pay his troops. Wary of Ferdinand's autocratic tendencies, his subjects were reluctant to trust him with a permanent mercenary army. The war with the Turks thus degenerated into a long and bloody stalemate that dragged on until the late seventeenth century.

Although Ferdinand was generally obliged to respect the constitutional liberties of his Danubian realms, the pressures of war compelled him to establish a central administration in Vienna to keep track of revenues. The privy council, treasury, and Bohemian and Hungarian chancelleries that he created came to form the nucleus of the bureaucratic structure of government through which the Austrian Hapsburgs bound their disparate kingdoms together. The multinational unity of Austria, Bohemia, and Hungary was to endure until the very end of Hapsburg rule in 1918.

The religious uncertainties loosed by the Protestant Reformation greatly complicated Ferdinand's efforts to unify the government of his lands. The Czech population of Bohemia was predominantly Protestant, Calvinism had spread widely among the sixteenth-century Hungarian nobility, and Austria had come to have a large Lutheran minority. Although a staunch Catholic, Ferdinand found it imprudent to insist too rigorously on religious conformity. In 1555, after

Charles V's abdication and his own accession to the German crown, Ferdinand helped negotiate the Peace of Augsburg, which permitted the German princes to choose between Catholicism and Lutheranism as the religion their people should follow. Ferdinand's son, Emperor Maximilian II, seemed at times strongly inclined to convert to Protestantism. He forbade publication of the conservative decrees of the Council of Trent since they increased papal authority, and he did little to promote the reforms of the Counter Reformation. Predictably, the number of religious dissenters increased steadily.

Not until the late sixteenth century did the

Above, a banquet celebrating the Peace of Westphalia (1648), which ended the Thirty Years' War. The host, Charles Gustavus, count palatine of Zweibrücken (standing in the foreground), became king of Sweden in 1654. The peace treaty marked the end of the Hapsburgs' predominance in Germany and forced them to consolidate their power over the hereditary lands, resulting in a great multinational state.

Left, some of the acts ratifying the Peace of Westphalia. Negotiations for peace began in 1644; the Swedes and German Protestant states met at Osnabrück, and the French and German Roman Catholic states convened at Münster. The peace restored the territorial status quo of 1618, with a few important exceptions. The Hapsburgs, for example, recognized the United Provinces of the Netherlands as an independent sovereign state and ceded some rights in Alsace to France; and Charles Louis, eldest son of the Winter King Frederick V, was restored to the Lower Palatinate, in the Rhineland area of Germany.

The empire's sword

During medieval times the Hapsburgs defended their lands and conducted wars with the help of locally recruited bands of militia. There was no fixed military organization or centralized administration. The Hapsburgs were dependent for military support on the whims of great lords, who could raise armies from their own retainers, and on the local estates, which normally cooperated only in return for large concessions. This situation did not change until 1560 when Ferdinand I established the Hofkriegsrat, a small advisory council for military affairs.

Albrecht von Wallenstein (right) was the mercenary on whom Ferdinand II relied most during the Thirty Years' War. He became duke of Friedland, indisputable head of the imperial army, and ruled almost like a sovereign prince from 1625 until 1634. A brilliant, charismatic administrator and strategist, his ultimate ambition was to be crowned king of Bohemia. After his death, army organization was centralized under the Hofkriegsrat, at that time the imperial war office.

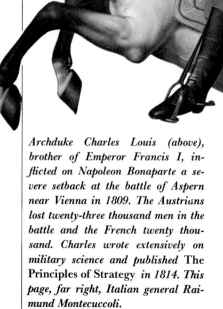

Archduke Charles Louis (above), brother of Emperor Francis I, inflicted on Napoleon Bonaparte a severe setback at the battle of Aspern near Vienna in 1809. The Austrians lost twenty-three thousand men in the battle and the French twenty thousand. Charles wrote extensively on military science and published The Principles of Strategy *in 1814. This page, far right, Italian general Raimund Montecuccoli.*

Above, one of the flags of the imperial army, with the Hapsburg eagle in the middle. Left, Austrian count Joseph Radetzky in the uniform of a Russian field marshal, painted by J. Neugebauer. One of the greatest defenders of the empire, Radetzky crushed the revolutionary and nationalist uprisings in Italy against Hapsburg rule in 1848–1849.

Above right, Prince Eugene of Savoy, astride his horse. He entered the service of Emperor Leopold I in 1683, after King Louis XIV of France had rejected him; as a brilliant general, he won many spectacular and daring victories over both the Turks and the French. He was also a generous patron of the arts. Left, Archduke Albert, who was victorious over the Italians at the battle of Custoza in 1866. An arch conservative, Albert was Emperor Francis Joseph's principal military adviser. He tried to reform the Austrian army in the 1870s, but was unable to stop the Austro-Hungarian Empire's military decline. Right, Franz von Hötzendorf, appointed chief of the Austrian General Staff in 1906.

Counter Reformation begin to make headway in the Austrian Hapsburg lands. Maximilian II's son Rudolf II, a devout Catholic, encouraged the Jesuits to promote a Catholic revival through education, preaching, and philanthropic services to the poor. Most of the archdukes were educated in Spain, and they brought back to Austria a taste for Spanish Catholicism, culture, and ceremonial. Rudolf II and his brothers sought to expel Protestant preachers from the towns, although they dared not provoke rebellion by attacking the religious liberties of the nobility. To conciliate the dominant Protestant elements in Hungary and Bohemia, Rudolf in 1609 granted both kingdoms a "Letter of Majesty" guaranteeing religious toleration.

Having been persuaded by the Jesuits to lead a counterattack on heresy throughout the Holy Roman Empire, the early seventeenth-century Hapsburgs propelled east-central Europe into the tragic conflagration known as the Thirty Years' War (1618–1648). As early as 1605, Rudolf II, judged a bit mad by his relatives, was replaced as ruler of the Austrian provinces by his bigoted Roman Catholic brother Matthias, who later also succeeded Rudolf as Holy Roman emperor. Matthias entrusted the guidance of the Hapsburgs' religious and political affairs to the

Near right, a detail of a Turkish musket abandoned during the siege of Vienna in 1683. The city was courageously defended by Count Ernst Rüdiger von Starhemberg until a relief army of twenty thousand men arrived under King John III Sobieski of Poland and Charles of Lorraine.

Left, Emperor Leopold I dressed as a shepherd. As a diversion from his military cares, Leopold frequented the opera and theater. He often dressed up in costume and participated in the lavish entertainments he arranged for the court. Above, a dinner given in honor of Leopold I's marriage to Margaret Theresa of Spain, painted by Jan Thomas in 1666. The two consorts are seated at the far end of the left table. By marrying his cousin, Leopold strengthened Austrian Hapsburg claims to the Spanish inheritance.

bishop of Vienna, Melchior Khlesl. In 1617, Archduke Ferdinand of Styria, an admirer of the Roman Catholic Jesuits, became king of Bohemia and promptly began to undermine the Protestants' position there. Ferdinand's tampering with Bohemia's liberties set off a powerful resistance movement among the Bohemian nobles, in which Protestant religious conviction, veneration of the local law, and incipient Czech nationalism mingled inseparably. In 1618, forcefully demonstrating their determination to resist oppression, the leaders of the Bohemian diet threw the Hapsburgs' representatives bodily out of a high window in the royal castle of Prague, onto a pile of dung below. This historic moment became known as the Defenestration of Prague.

The Bohemian challenge was met by the now-deposed king Ferdinand, who had succeeded Matthias as Holy Roman emperor in 1619. Ferdinand relied on the financial backing of his Spanish relatives, entrusted his conscience to his Jesuit confessor, and arrested Bishop Khlesl when that ecclesiastic ventured to suggest the need for compromise. Meanwhile the Bohemian rebels assured themselves of the support of the German Protestant princes and elected Frederick of the Palatinate, the Winter King, as their new ruler.

Above, a detail of the siege of Vienna by the Turks in 1683. The Turkish army advanced on the Austrian capital unresisted and besieged it for sixty days before Leopold I's hastily gathered relief force came to the rescue. The Turks were defeated and Vienna was spared from the horrors of looting, rape, and fire. The victory marked the start of a major decline in power for the Ottoman Turks. The Hapsburgs soon ousted them from Hungary and Transylvania.

Left, the saddle of the Turkish vizier Kara Mustafa, abandoned with the rest of his luxurious possessions during his escape from Vienna in 1683. Mustafa paid for his greed and incompetence with his head, which was presented to the Turkish sultan Mohammed IV on a silver dish later that year.

Prince Eugene

Prince Eugene of Savoy was the son of Olympia, the notorious niece of the French cardinal and statesman Mazarin and an intimate of Louis XIV of France. When Olympia became involved in a poison scandal at the French court and left France in 1680, Eugene's chances for a brilliant career seemed doomed; Louis XIV refused Eugene's enthusiastic requests to join the army. Eugene then offered his services to Emperor Leopold I in 1683, just before the siege of Vienna. They were graciously accepted, and Eugene soon proved to be the greatest general of his era, defeating both the Turks and the French in a series of memorable battles. Eugene was not only a master strategist, but also a distinguished patron of the arts. In addition to commissioning Austria's greatest architects, Johann Lucas von Hildebrandt and Johann Bernhard Fischer von Erlach, to design two palaces for him, he also amassed a brilliant collection of paintings and sculpture.

Top right, a detail of a decorative wrought-iron gateway at Belvedere Palace in Vienna. Prince Eugene's coat of arms can be seen on either side. In 1707 a cabinetmaker, Leonhard Sattler, made this "Turkish bed" (below) for Eugene. The bed, now in the abbey of St. Florian, is a masterpiece of Austrian Baroque. Right, a detail of a marble sculpture of the prince, crafted by Balthasar Permoser.

Left, the façade of the Upper Belvedere, part of Belvedere Palace. This summer residence was built by Johann Lucas von Hildebrandt between 1721 and 1722 for Prince Eugene of Savoy. Eugene used the large pavilion in the Upper Belvedere for entertaining his guests; his actual residence was in the Lower Belvedere. Hildebrandt also designed another of Eugene's residences—the Schlosshof (immediately below), built ca. 1725. Its location in the Marchfeld, a plain east of Vienna, was ideal for Eugene's hunting parties.

The Gold Cabinet (immediately above), in Prince Eugene's Winter Palace in Vienna, was so named because of its extravagant gilded decoration. The interiors of Eugene's residences were decorated in the opulent yet delicate Austrian Rococo style that dominated aristocratic taste during the eighteenth century. The palaces reflected not only the prince's love of art and passion for architectural innovation, but also the glory of his military career. He took an interest in all the details of his artistic commissions and was even heard discussing them on the battlefield. Right, an interior of the Schlosshof, revealing Prince Eugene's chessboard.

Early in 1620 an army raised by Ferdinand's German Catholic allies inflicted a decisive defeat on the Bohemians in the Battle of the White Mountain, and Frederick was forced to flee. About half the lands of the Bohemian nobility were handed over to supporters of the Hapsburg cause. German as well as Italian, Spanish, French, and even Irish families became great landowners in Bohemia, and the native Czech aristocracy was decimated. In 1621, Ferdinand compelled all Protestant ministers to leave Bohemia, and in 1627 he ordered the entire population of the country to choose between Catholicism and exile. More than thirty thousand native families left the

kingdom. Finally, in a series of decrees in 1627–1628, Ferdinand proclaimed that Bohemia was no longer an elective monarchy: The land was reduced to a hereditary property of the House of Hapsburg.

Victory over the Bohemian Protestant aristocracy tempted Ferdinand to complete the task begun a century before by his ancestor Charles V: the transformation of the shadowy power of the Holy Roman emperor into effective sovereignty and the imposition of religious uniformity on all of Germany. The brilliant and arrogant leader of Ferdinand's mercenary army, Albrecht von Wallenstein, defeated an alliance of Protestant princes, carrying Hapsburg power to

In the late seventeenth century, the Hapsburgs fought against the Ottoman Turks (two scenes, facing page, far left), who launched a major offensive into central Europe, only to be driven out of Hungary. Top scene, an imperial commander, Duke Charles of Lorraine, at the battle of Pressburg, 1683. The tapestry was made at Nancy, France, between 1709 and 1718. Bottom scene, the "second" battle of Mohács, 1687, in which the imperial forces were led by Duke Charles.

Center, the primarily Baroque castle of Forchtenstein, protected by a double fortified wall. It was reinforced in the seventeenth century in preparation for a Turkish attack. Above, a Viennese print showing the Hapsburg conquest of a Turkish camp in Dubica, Bosnia, in 1688. Left, a portrait of Margrave Ludwig Wilhelm of Baden, who was given the honorary title Lieutenant of the Empire. Like Prince Eugene, he often wore Turkish dress.

the shores of the Baltic. In 1629, without consulting the German princes or the Reichstag (the imperial diet), Ferdinand proclaimed the Edict of Restitution, restoring all property taken from the Catholic Church since 1555. With this act, Ferdinand had gone too far, for even the German Catholic princes now were alarmed at the Hapsburgs' overweening power; to the Protestant princes Ferdinand appeared as a threat not only to religious liberty but also to property rights.

Cardinal Richelieu, the French king's chief minister, encouraged King Gustavus Adolphus of Sweden to rally the German Protestants against the Haps-burgs. A superb general, Gustavus Adolphus outmaneuvered Wallenstein with seeming invincibility until he fell in battle in 1632. Wallenstein's subsequent attempts to negotiate an end to the war independently of Ferdinand culminated in the former's asassination in 1634.

The war gradually became an open military struggle, with France and Sweden in opposition to the Austrian and Spanish Hapsburgs. Devastation, followed by plague, typhus, and witchcraft panics, engulfed a large part of Germany and Bohemia. In 1643 French forces defeated the Spanish Hapsburg army in present-day Belgium, but not until 1648 was the

The imperial army

The imperial army's fame and solidarity in the sixteenth and seventeenth centuries were extraordinary considering the motley composition of the force. Although Ferdinand I's military council, the Hofkriegsrat, had assembled a small permanent army of about nine thousand men at the end of the sixteenth century and the empire's military frontier system was improved and expanded in the seventeenth century, the Hapsburg rulers continued throughout the eighteenth century to depend on assembled regiments of mercenary armies. The system was successful because large numbers of minor nobles and aristocrats were always willing to seek their fortune by fighting for the imperial cause. Once they had sworn their oath of loyalty to the emperor, they normally remained obedient to his commands and could even be relied on to fight their own countrymen. The soldiers of the lower ranks, enlisted primarily from the Alpine provinces, proved to be equally well disciplined, helping to create an efficient army.

The three miniatures (near right) depict officers in the imperial army: top to bottom, an Austrian officer holding a miniature of his wife, an artillery officer in 1780, and an officer from the cuirassier regiment Franz III. Top center, a hand-colored pen and ink drawing (1777) of the imperial pikemen performing a military exercise called the "Spanish Horse." The soldiers would rest their lances against a big wooden beam forming a barrier against attack.

This page, center right, Field Marshal Columban von Bender, who fought in the Low Countries between 1790 and 1795. Bottom right, an Austrian official adorning a snuff box, 1770. Facing page, bottom left, an officer in Prince Eugene of Savoy's dragoon regiment of heavily armed troopers. Facing page, far right, top to bottom, a field marshal wearing the Cross of the Order of Maria Theresa; an infantry officer of 1770; Emperor Leopold II dressed in a dragoon's uniform (1790); and Field Marshal Franz Ludwig von Neugebauer, who died in 1808. These miniatures were a favorite art form of the eighteenth-century aristocracy.

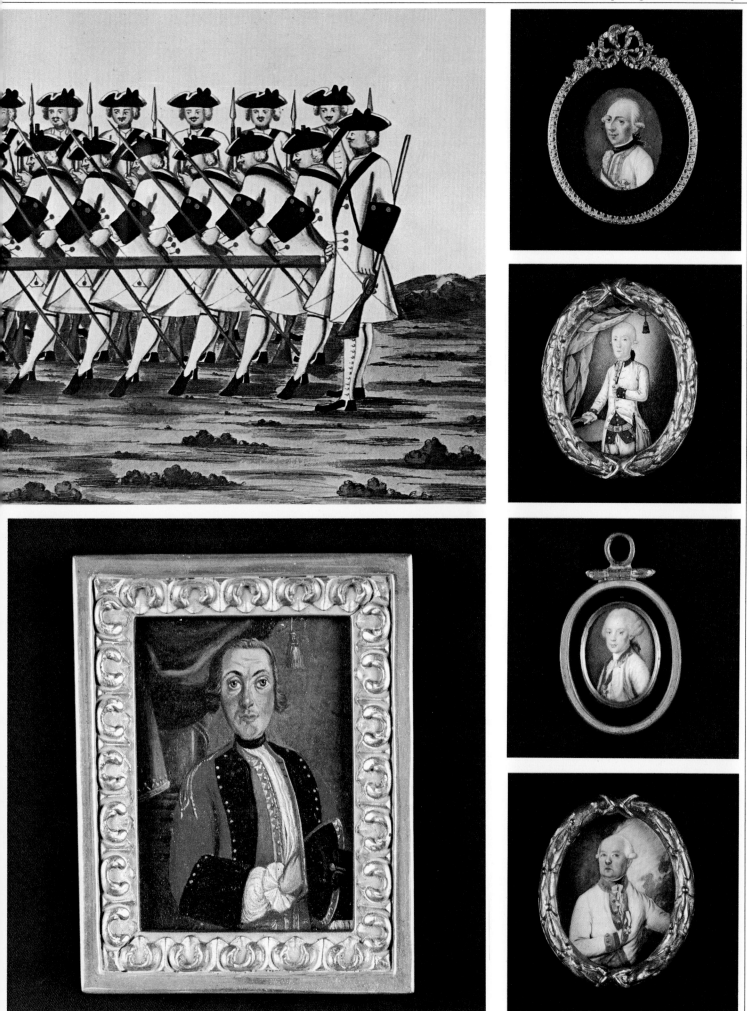

horrible war finally brought to an end with the Peace of Westphalia.

Defeat in the Thirty Years' War proved to be the decisive consideration in the Hapsburgs' bid for imperial power over Germany and Europe. Although Ferdinand II and his successor, Ferdinand III (reigned 1637–1657), had openly proclaimed that the German princes were their subjects and—against the advice of even their Spanish cousins—attempted to impose Roman Catholicism as the sole religion of the empire, the Peace of Westphalia allowed each of Germany's many sovereign units the freedom to choose its own belief. Much of Germany thereafter fell under French political influence and only in their own lands—Austria, Bohemia, and Hungary—could the Hapsburgs claim absolute rule and enforcement of religious conformity. From this time onward the Austrian Hapsburgs were compelled to look to the Danubian basin rather than to Germany for the fulfillment of their political aspirations.

The Hapsburgs' turn to the east after the Thirty Years' War coincided with a dramatic revival of the military capabilities of the Ottoman Turks. In 1658 Transylvania fell under direct Turkish rule, and the Hungarian and Austrian capitals of Pressburg (present-day Bratislava) and Vienna were threatened. The new Hapsburg emperor, Leopold I (reigned 1657–1705), repelled the Ottoman attack, but fearing a lengthy and expensive war, made peace in 1664 on the basis of the territorial status quo. The Hungarian nobles, who longed to reunite their country and assure its independence, were so enraged when Leopold failed to press his advantage that they revolted against the Hapsburgs in 1670 and again in 1678. Ominous signs of an ever more menacing Turkish assault, coinciding with an attack on the Holy Roman Empire by Louis XIV of France, persuaded Leopold to offer the Hungarians new guarantees of their liberties.

In 1683, Sultan Mohammed IV and his grand vizier, Kara Mustafa, sent an army of two hundred thousand warriors and camp-followers against Vienna. In his declaration of war the sultan advised Leopold to convert to Islam, "or else I will give order to consume you with fire, . . . put your sacred priests to the plow, and expose the breasts of your matrons to be sucked by dogs." Although Leopold fled Vienna, leaving a garrison of a mere ten thousand, Kara Mustafa delivered an ultimatum to the city, still hoping to persuade it to surrender and pay a tribute instead of being stormed and plundered by the Turkish soldiers. The siege, lasting sixty days, reduced the Viennese to eating rats and leather belts. Leopold made judicious use of the interval, however, to rally

Top, the seal of the Turkish sultan Mustafa II, on the document ratifying the Treaty of Karlowitz, 1699. Mustafa recognized Emperor Leopold I as sovereign over Hungary and Transylvania in this treaty. Immediately above, Prince Eugene of Savoy at the battle in which he captured Belgrade (in present-day Yugoslavia) from the Turks in 1717. Hostilities with Turkey resumed soon after the Treaty of Karlowitz: Mustafa II was deposed in 1703 and replaced by Ahmed III, a ruler of great ability, who exploited the Hapsburgs' vulnerability during the War of the Spanish Succession.

In 1716, Prince Eugene of Savoy defeated Turkish defending forces at Fort Peterwardein on the Danube (left). This victory was followed by the reoccupation of Belgrade by imperial troops in 1717 and a peace treaty with the Turks in 1718. Below, a section of D. Coho's view of Vienna in 1690, shortly after the Austrian capital had recovered from the Turkish siege in 1683. The strongly fortified walls that kept the Turks at bay are in the foreground. The angular bastions atop the walls were specially designed both for firing and for defense against cannon balls (the balls would bounce off the corner walls).

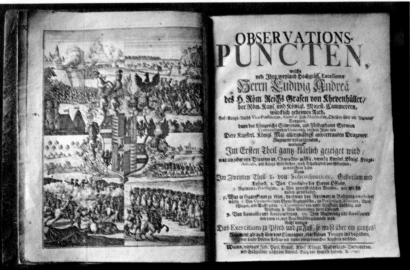

aid from various German princes and the Polish king John III Sobieski, who joined with him to rout the Turks.

After the relief of Vienna, Leopold's generals took the offensive, and over the next twenty years Hapsburg power was extended far down the Danube, to Belgrade and even beyond. All of Turkish Hungary was conquered and devastated. The vanquished country was placed under Hapsburg hereditary rule: Leopold compelled the Hungarian diet to renounce the principle of elective monarchy for as long as the male line of the Hapsburg dynasty continued. The wide stretches of Hungary that military operations

had depopulated were eventually resettled with foreign immigrants—mostly Germans and Serbs—whose arrival created nationalistic tensions that bore bitter fruit in the nineteenth and twentieth centuries.

By the time Leopold and the sultan signed the Treaty of Karlowitz in 1699, Hungary had become a multinational bastion of a new Hapsburg empire along the entire middle stretch of the Danube. Within four years, the Hungarian nobility was sufficiently fearful of Hapsburg domination to organize a rebellion under Francis II Rákóczy, a powerful magnate and ally of Louis XIV. Hungarian resistance continued until 1711, when Rákóczy finally surren-

Above far left, an ivory statuette of Emperor Charles VI on horseback, by Matthias Steinle. The figure on the ground represents a peasant dressed in traditional costume. Below far left, a manual on military exercises. It was published in Vienna during Charles VI's reign by Count Ludwig Andreas von Klevenhüller for the regiment of the imperial dragoons.

Left, the room in Rastatt Palace where Prince Eugene of Savoy and his adversary, the French general Marshall Villars, signed the Peace of Rastatt in 1714. This treaty officially ended the war between Emperor Charles VI and King Louis XIV of France over who should accede to the Spanish throne. Fighting, however, sporadically continued until 1720.

Above, a finely made eighteenth-century silver medal depicting Joseph I. Below, part of the Pragmatic Sanction (1713), to which Charles VI's seal is attached. The declaration stipulated that in the absence of male heirs, the eldest daughter would inherit the Hapsburg lands. Charles, then childless, had wanted to ensure a peaceful accession to his throne.

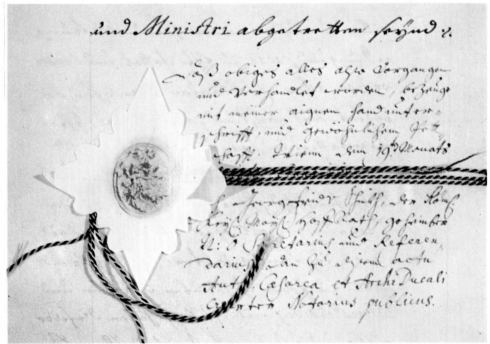

dered, but only after suffering repeated defeats in battle and the outbreak of a plague to which one sixth of the country's population fell victim.

Leopold I, under whom the Austrian Hapsburgs had won such spectacular victories, almost immediately resigned himself to the hopelessness of ever reviving the Holy Roman Empire. He also inured himself to the oppressiveness of the bureaucracy he ruled. During his reign the Austrian officialdom aimed even more openly at creating a centralized state, and plans to promote the economic unification and development of the Danubian basin were seriously advanced for the first time.

While winning their new empire in southeastern Europe, the Austrian Hapsburgs also watched the affairs of western Europe, but more with an aim of helping England maintain the balance of power against Louis XIV's France than with any hope of reasserting the nominal power of the Holy Roman emperor. Yet in 1700 there appeared a final opportunity to revive something of the substance of Charles V's dynastic strategies. The feeble-minded Spanish Hapsburg king Charles II had at last died without heirs, thus ending the Spanish Hapsburg line, which had been in precipitous decline since the end of the Thirty Years' War. Although in his will Charles II

Left, the garden façade of Schönbrunn Palace outside of Vienna, completed in 1750 during the reign of Maria Theresa.

Below left, a coin bearing a likeness of Maria Theresa. Although her long reign (1740–1780) was punctuated by costly wars, Austria prospered economically.

Above left, Maria Theresa and family on the terrace of Schönbrunn Palace. Her husband, Francis I, is seated on the left and Joseph, heir to the throne, stands in the middle.

Above, the imperial family at a concert. The young Mozart was among the many famous musicians to play before Maria Theresa in this era of splendor.

had bequeathed his empire to Louis XIV's grandson, Duke Philip of Anjou, Leopold I saw Charles' death as an opportunity to re-establish the unity of the Hapsburg dynasty. He therefore advanced his son, Archduke Charles, as a rival candidate, demanding an equitable partition of the Spanish inheritance.

Louis XIV's rejection of this demand and his insistence that Anjou receive Spain and all its possessions, thereby decisively altering the balance of power in France's favor, plunged Europe into the War of the Spanish Succession (1702). In this conflict, the Austrian Hapsburgs were joined in a coalition with England and the Dutch Republic. Decisive victories by the English general, the duke of Marlborough, and by Leopold's commander, Prince Eugene of Savoy, forced Louis XIV into a defensive position. By 1711, when the archduke Charles became Emperor Charles VI following the deaths of Leopold I and his son Joseph I, a Hapsburg rather than a Bourbon domination of Europe seemed likely. England's defection from the alliance, however, forced the commencement of peace negotiations and restored the balance of power. Philip of Anjou received Spain and most of its overseas empire, while Charles VI added to the Austrian Hapsburgs' possessions such valuable territories in Europe as the Spanish Netherlands (modern

Pandours

The first major appearance of light troops in European warfare occurred during the War of Austrian Succession (1740–1748). Maria Theresa called upon the Pandours to help defend against Frederick II of Prussia and his allies. These border troops, which had long been part of Austria's defenses against the Turks, were very effective in protecting the army's main line and in reconnaissance and ambushing.

Above right, a Prussian version of an Austrian Pandour. This light cavalryman in the army of King Frederick II is dressed in Serbian costume. His large, heavy curved saber is particularly suitable for use on horseback. Below, a Prussian cavalryman. This type of soldier never became a dominant force in the Prussian army and disappeared during the Napoleonic Wars.

Belgium), Milan, the kingdom of Naples, and Sardinia.

Emperor Charles VI faced a situation not unlike that of the recently deceased Charles II of Spain: He lacked a direct heir. To avoid a conflict between claimants as well as a partition of his lands after his death, Charles VI signed the Pragmatic Sanction in 1713. This significant decree was to alter the empire: The Austrian Hapsburg lands, whose unity Leopold I had effectively defended, were declared to form a single indivisible state that was to pass to a single heir—male if possible but female if necessary. With this act, the concept of the Austrian Hapsburg lands constituting a modern state—rather than a conglomeration of provinces that could be divided to suit the convenience of heirs and assigns—had come into existence. In 1717 Charles at last acquired an heir: a girl, Maria Theresa, who would have to fight to defend the integrity of the Pragmatic Sanction.

Charles VI spent the rest of his reign negotiating with the other monarchs of Europe to win approval for the Pragmatic Sanction. The diets of the Hapsburg realms and the powers of Europe were naturally reluctant to forego the opportunity to profit from a disputed succession to the Hapsburgs' lands; Charles therefore was obliged to retreat from the rigid policy of centralization that Leopold I had pursued before him. In the end, only the Hungarians recognized the Pragmatic Sanction unreservedly as law—in return for Charles' solemn promise to rule Hungary according to its ancient statutes and liberties.

In 1740 Charles VI caught a chill while on a hunting expedition and died shortly thereafter. Maria Theresa was now twenty-three years old and married to the duke of Lorraine, Francis Stephen (later Emperor Francis I). As provided by the Pragmatic Sanction, she inherited the Hapsburgs' hereditary lands in Austria and Germany, the Austrian Netherlands, the crowns of Hungary and Bohemia, and several Italian duchies.

Her position, however, was initially very weak, largely as a result of several blunders her father had committed at the end of his reign. Despite his limited financial resources and the comparative modesty of his military might, Charles VI had become embroiled in a single-handed fight with the Bourbons on two fronts, had intervened in the War of the Polish Succession, and had drifted into a calamitous war with Turkey. In the process he lost a great deal of prestige and some valuable territory, including the kingdom of Naples in 1738 and Serbia—with its strategic fortress at Belgrade—in 1739. When Maria Theresa succeeded her father, she found the Hapsburg finances in shambles (debts were enormous and most of the royal

Field Marshal Count Leopold von Daun (above) was the imperial general who defeated Frederick II of Prussia at the battle of Kolín (near Prague) in 1757. Right, Frederick II of Prussia. Below right, Austrian military regulations of 1759, signed by Maria Theresa. Immediately below, an early eighteenth-century Prussian headdress.

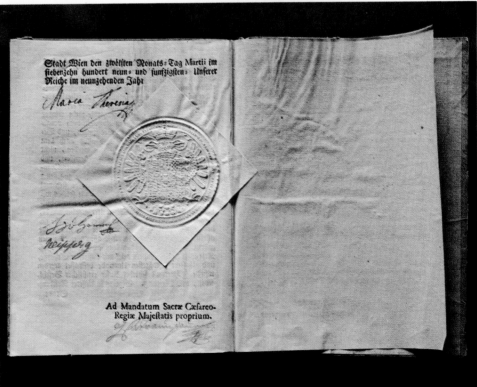

domains had been mortgaged), the army at half strength and unpaid, and the ministers at her disposal aged and ineffectual.

One of the most serious and persistent threats to the Hapsburg Empire during Maria Theresa's reign was posed by Prussia's newly crowned Frederick II (the Great), who was determined to raise his German state to the status of a great power. To this end, Frederick invaded the fertile, mineral-rich, and densely populated Bohemian land of Silesia—one of the Hapsburgs' most valuable possessions, accounting for about one quarter of all the direct taxes collected from Bohemia and Austria. Although Maria Theresa's army tried to resist the advance of the extremely well-trained Prussian forces, the Austrians were eventually defeated at the battle of Mollwitz in April of 1741; in October, Maria Theresa was forced to sign a treaty in which she ceded Lower Silesia to Prussia.

Charles Albert, the elector of Bavaria, took advantage of Maria Theresa's evident weakness and, with the support of France, which led the anti-Hapsburg movement, challenged her succession: In July of 1741 he invaded Austria in conjunction with the French. The War of Succession that followed (1741–1748) was a long, drawn-out affair. Charles Albert succeeded in capturing the Bohemian capital of Prague and was crowned king of Bohemia and Holy Roman emperor in 1742. With the exception of Hungary, where Maria Theresa had been crowned queen in 1741, the nobility of the provinces occupied by the Prussians and Bavarians refused to come to her support. To the south, Spanish troops were attempting to reclaim Hapsburg territory in northern Italy. In the spring of 1744, France declared war on Austria and the next year defeated the Hapsburgs' allies—the British and

Right, the façade of Schönbrunn Palace, the Hapsburgs' summer residence, as viewed from its park. Leopold I decided to build this palace for his son Joseph in 1683 and commissioned Johann Bernhard Fischer von Erlach to design it. In 1728, Emperor Charles VI bought the palace from Joseph's widow and employed Fischer von Erlach's son Joseph to extend it. Schönbrunn received its final additions from Nicolaus Pacassi, Maria Theresa's architect, in the 1740s. Above right, a partial view of Schönbrunn, as seen from its gardens. The beautiful gardens surrounding the palace were planned and realized during the first half of the eighteenth century.

Above, a framed message signed by Maria Theresa, which accompanied a gift sent to one of her subjects. A very motherly and kind woman, she corresponded voluminously with her friends and her sixteen children. Right, Maria Theresa being shown pictures brought to her from Italy by her favorite daughter, Maria Christina, and her daughter's husband, Prince Albert of Saxony.

Left, an interior of the Hofburg, decorated and furnished in the Rococo style. Originally built as a medieval fortress, the Hofburg witnessed several additions by the Hapsburgs in each century. By the nineteenth century it included government buildings, a national library, a riding school, a court chapel, and the Hapsburgs' main residence. Above, one of the many clocks in the Hofburg. Note the automated figures that moved with the rest of the mechanism; clocks such as these were popular eighteenth-century curios.

Dutch—in the Austrian Netherlands.

Yet all was not lost for Austria. Maria Theresa's forces recaptured Prague and saw her crowned queen of Bohemia in 1743; in 1745, upon the death of Charles Albert, her husband was crowned Emperor Francis I; and in Italy the Hapsburgs were forced to cede only small areas to the Spanish Bourbons. There was no overcoming Frederick the Great, however, and Silesia was not recovered. This led to the emergence of Prussia as a future rival to Hapsburg power in Germany. (To counterbalance the loss of Silesia, Maria Theresa took part in the first partition of Poland in 1772, acquiring the populous territory hence-forth known as Galicia.) The contest was viewed as a defensive victory for the Hapsburgs and as proof that the empire had been able to establish a certain cohesive unity among its lands.

To ensure prosperity and efficiency—essential in light of the military challenge presented by Frederick the Great's Prussia—Maria Theresa cautiously continued the transformation of her lands into a bureaucratic state. She promoted education, capitalistic agriculture, and manufacturing and lessened the rigors of serfdom by relieving the peasants of such onerous feudal obligations to their lords as forced labor, thereby reducing the power of the nobility.

Above left, a coin struck in 1786 during the reign of Joseph II, Maria Theresa's eldest son. The imperial crown and the Collar of the Golden Fleece are incorporated into the central emblem. The legend around the edge lists Joseph's main titles in a type of shorthand. From 1780 to 1790 Joseph II (left) tried to reform almost every aspect of the Hapsburg Empire according to the rational ideals of the Enlightenment.

Cultural life also flourished, as evidenced by the magnificent Baroque and Rococo buildings constructed in Austria during this time. Musically, Austria was host to such composers as Haydn and Mozart, chief exponents of the Viennese, or classical, school.

Under Maria Theresa the central bureaucracy became in some respects more powerful than the provincial diets, and the revenues at the government's disposal increased rapidly. But Maria Theresa realized that augmenting the power of the central government would antagonize entrenched interests and thus introduced changes as carefully as possible.

Hungary, for example, continued to be governed largely by its nobility, and throughout the empire aristocrats formed the leading elements in the bureaucracy. Until the Hapsburgs' final collapse, in fact, the loyalty of the higher aristocracy was a bastion of the dynasty's power.

Her son and heir, Joseph II, while sharing his mother's fundamental political objectives, was anticlerical and impatient. It might well be said of this "enlightened autocrat" that he was determined, through radical reform, to make his subjects happy and useful to the state—whether they liked it or not. He would brook no criticism of his authoritarian

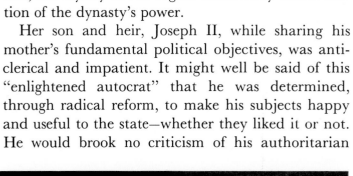

Above, Emperor Joseph II on a white horse, in the foreground. This study is unusually martial in tone; while Joseph often wore military uniforms as everyday dress, he basically viewed himself as a legislator rather than a warrior. Above right, a detail of a portrait of Joseph II (right) and his brother, later Leopold II (left), in Rome, painted by Pompeo Batoni in 1769. Right, a fireworks ceremony at the Gloriette, at Schönbrunn Palace, in honor of Joseph II.

This allegorical print (above left), depicting freely worshiping representatives of various religions, refers to Joseph II's Edict of Toleration (1781). The edict ordered an end to repression and discrimination against adherents of the Lutheran, Calvinist, and Greek Orthodox faiths. Left, the inner courtyard of St. Florian Abbey on the Danube.

government. As his brother Leopold observed, "He tolerates no contradiction and is imbued with arbitrary, brutal principles and the most severe, brutal, and violent despotism."

Characteristically, Joseph admired and envied the centralized states, governed by absolute monarchs, that were emerging in many parts of Europe. Although it was clearly impossible to create a coherent, unified state out of the scattered lands he ruled, Joseph was set on making the Hapsburg Empire more homogeneous. He introduced administrative reforms into the duchy of Milan and the Austrian Netherlands and welded the regions of Austria, Bohemia, and

Hungary into one country with a central administration in Vienna. In doing so he demoted Bohemia and Hungary from their special status as kingdoms. He refused to be crowned in either country and actually moved the Crown of St. Stephen—the Hungarians' sacred symbol of national independence—from the Hungarian capital of Pressburg to Vienna. To promote bureaucratic uniformity within the empire, Joseph proclaimed German the sole language of all official business, except in Lombardy and the Austrian Netherlands. He also imposed strict censorship. Mozart's *Marriage of Figaro*, for example, was harshly received when first performed in Vienna in 1786 be-

Above, the Benedictine Abbey of Melk, rebuilt by Jakob Prandtauer in the early eighteenth century, seen from across the Danube. Above right, a detail of a ceremonial robe decorated with typical Hapsburg motifs, such as the two-headed eagle and the imperial crown. Right, a portrait of Leopold II, Holy Roman emperor from 1790 to 1792.

cause of its criticism of the aristocracy, and by implication, the monarchy.

In 1781, Joseph abolished personal serfdom, in part to increase the revenues flowing into his treasury. All peasants living in the Hapsburg Empire were now allowed to marry, pursue any trade or profession, or move to another estate without first obtaining their lord's permission. Joseph also issued decrees guaranteeing hereditary tenure of property to peasants. By these measures he hoped that the peasants—who constituted the majority of his subjects—would grow richer and pay more taxes. For similar self-interested motives he encouraged trade and industry within the Hapsburg Empire by a variety of measures that included religious toleration for Protestants and Jews, subsidies for new enterprises, tariff barriers to discourage foreign imports, and an improved postal system and road network.

Joseph II did not live long enough to crush the opposition he provoked by his innovations. His foreign policy proved to be basically a failure: The Austrian Netherlands were in open revolt against Hapsburg rule by 1787, Hungary was organizing an uprising by 1788, and for the next three years, the imperial treasury was drained by a needless and expensive war, fought with Russia against Turkey, which ended in compromise. The epitaph he composed on his deathbed was understandably bitter: "Here lies Joseph II, who was unfortunate in all his enterprises."

His brother and successor, Leopold II, spent most of his two-year reign (1790–1792) making large concessions to the interests offended by Joseph's reforms. He recognized the estates of his various lands as "the pillars of the monarchy," pacified the Hungarians by consenting to be crowned their king, and restored order in the Austrian Netherlands. Although Leopold II had reforming tendencies and initially supported the humanitarian ideals of the French Revolution (1789–1799), he took alarm at the declining strength of the French monarchy. As brother of Marie Antoinette, he allowed his court to become a rallying point for émigrés from Revolutionary France. Because France was growing stronger militarily as a result of the Revolution and thereby threatened to upset the balance of power in Europe, Leopold was forced to become more reactionary in his political considerations. In February of 1792, the emperor entered into a defensive alliance with Prussia against the French; three months later, shortly after Leopold's death, France declared war on Austria, beginning what was to be almost twenty-five years of continual warfare among the major European powers.

From 1792 to 1835 the fortunes of the Hapsburgs were in the hands of Leopold II's son Francis, crowned Holy Roman emperor as Francis II and king of both the Bohemians and Hungarians. Not a particularly intelligent or energetic ruler, he at first left the affairs of state in the care of his former tutor, the conservative Count Franz Colloredo. As the impact of the French Revolution began to be felt with increasing force throughout Europe, however, he was forced to become more active.

In 1793 King Louis XVI and Queen Marie Antoinette of France were executed by the Jacobins, a radical republican group formed during the Revolution. Francis was profoundly shocked by this challenge to the established monarchical order, particularly as Marie Antoinette was his aunt. When the police discovered two minor Jacobin conspiracies in Vienna and Hungary a year later, Francis' fears of revolution and its attendant evils, democracy and republicanism, were strongly reinforced, and he became a thoroughgoing reactionary. Bitterly hostile to the Revolution, he hired an army of informers to report on anybody suspected of trying to infiltrate revolutionary ideas into the monarchy and imposed a censorship which became progressively more strict.

During the persistent warfare that occurred between 1792 and 1815, the Hapsburg Empire found

Above, Francis of Hapsburg, last emperor of the Holy Roman Empire (as Francis II) and first emperor of Austria (as Francis I). From his accession as Holy Roman emperor in 1792 until the Congress of Vienna in 1815, Francis was almost constantly at war with France. Below, Viennese volunteers assembling to depart for war in 1797. Austria paid for its resistance to the great French leader Napoleon Bonaparte with a humiliating series of defeats and the loss of much territory, including the Austrian Netherlands and Lombardy. Right, an imperial procession en route to St. Stephen's Cathedral in Vienna, where Francis was crowned Holy Roman emperor.

Right, the meeting between Francis II (left), Napoleon (right), and the Russian czar Alexander I (background), after the battle of Austerlitz in 1805, in which the Austrians suffered a crushing defeat. Below right, three scenes of the Napoleonic Wars: upper left, the Grande Armée entering Vienna in 1805; lower left, French troops lining up along the Danube near Vienna before the battle of Wagram, 1809; right, the French bombardment of Vienna in 1809.

Facing page, above, a detail of the battle of Aspern, near Vienna, in 1809. It was during this struggle that Archduke Charles Louis, brother of Francis I, gave Napoleon his most severe setback before Napoleon's disastrous Russian campaign of 1812. Immediately below and facing page, far right, two pontoniers, army specialists in the construction of pontoon bridges.

itself to be the most heavily involved of the continental European powers. It was plagued by the military exploits of Napoleon Bonaparte, the brilliant Corsican who rose to power in the French army in the mid-1790s and effectively ruled France from 1799 until 1814. The main areas of conflict in the first war between Austria and France, the War of the First Coalition (1792–1797), involved the Spanish Netherlands and Italy. By 1794 the French had gained complete control of the Netherlands, and by 1796 Napoleon Bonaparte's campaign had wrested the northern Italian cities of Milan and Mantua from Austrian rule. Although Francis was forced to make concessions, they were minimal, for the principal Hapsburg territories were retained.

In 1804 Francis prudently assumed a new title—Emperor Francis I of Austria—to protect Austria's imperial position in the face of the growing power of Napoleon. During the War of the Third Coalition (1805–1807), though, Austria lost so many territories that the once-uncontested power of the Hapsburg Empire was virtually eradicated. After subjecting Austria to the harsh terms of the Treaty of Pressburg in late 1805—in which the Hapsburgs were forced to cede areas of Germany and Italy—Napoleon, recently crowned emperor of France, created the Confederation of the Rhine under his protection. At the same time, he dissolved the vanquished Holy Roman Empire, thus completing a process that had begun as early as the reign of Ferdinand I.

In 1809 Francis I's fortunes took a turn for the better when he appointed a prince from the Rhineland, Klemens von Metternich, as his foreign minister. Metternich, who had ample diplomatic experience and prided himself on understanding Napoleon's character, steered Francis in the direction of an alliance with Napoleon. In 1810, at Metternich's behest, Francis' daughter Marie Louise married Napoleon, thus providing Austria with a new but short-lived ally and a brief respite from war. Although in

The three most influential delegates at the Congress of Vienna were (facing page, left to right) Count Talleyrand, Napoleon's ex-foreign minister; Prince Metternich, foreign minister of the Austrian Empire; and Viscount Castlereagh, British foreign secretary. Britain was the only major power never defeated by Napoleon.

Left, a painting depicting Francis I and Austrian statesman Metternich passing the Vosges mountain range in northeastern France on July 2, 1815. The artist is Johann Nepomuk Höchle. Immediately below, the famous room in the Ballhausplatz, Prince Metternich's residence in Vienna, where in 1815 the delegates to the Congress of Vienna carried out their deliberations.

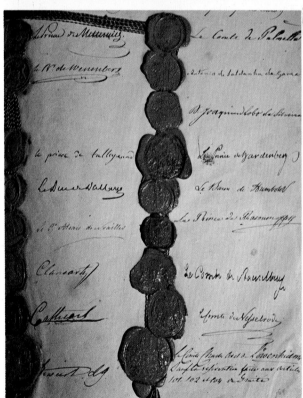

Immediately above, the last page of the Treaty of Vienna (June 1815), revealing the seals and signatures of the most prominent delegates. The 121 articles were the product of nine months of negotiation and established a balance of power in Europe that remained virtually intact until the Crimean War.

the War of 1812, the Hapsburg Empire managed to remain neutral, the following year, after Napoleon's rejection of Austria's demand for a return of lost territories, the Austrians entered the War of Liberation on the side of the anti-French alliance. By March of 1814 the allies had taken Paris and forced Napoleon's abdication from the French throne.

Once the Bourbon king Louis XVIII had been restored to the throne in April of 1814, Metternich did a great deal to re-establish Francis' shattered prestige. In September of 1814 he organized the largest peace conference ever held in Europe—the Congress of Vienna. Napoleon had so altered the map of Europe that almost every boundary and frontier had to be redrawn.

The Congress of Vienna lasted until June of 1815, and by the end of the year, after Napoleon's final defeat at Waterloo and his return to exile on the island of St. Helena, the Austrian Empire was almost one and one half times as large as when Metternich became foreign minister in 1809. It now covered present-day Austria, Hungary, Czechoslovakia, and parts of modern Romania, Yugoslavia, Italy, Poland, and the Soviet Union. Austria's influence on German affairs had been increased and its hold on Italy restored. But perhaps an even more significant result

was the establishment of what is now called the "Metternich system": a Europe ruled by monarchs who vigilantly suppressed symptoms of revolution, denied their subjects civil liberties and representative government, and rejected the demands of emergent nationalism. Their aim was to maintain the status quo within their own countries and a balance of power between nations.

The remainder of Francis' reign (1815–1835) was far from uneventful. Modern nationalism was awakening among the Czechs, Croats, Serbs, Romanians, and Hungarians; the entire period from 1815 to 1848 is often referred to as "the springtime of the peoples." National consciousness was promoted by the organization of scholarly and literary societies devoted to studying the cultural traditions of the various nationalities and by the creation of modern literary languages for these peoples; patriotism often was encouraged as a means of providing a popular basis for resisting further encroachments by the Hapsburgs' centralized bureaucratic state. This was also the age in which Austrian music reached its culmination in Beethoven and Schubert. Beethoven, who never made any secret of his republican sympathies, was faithfully patronized by Viennese aristocrats who recognized his genius and excused his political and social eccentricities.

At the same time, liberal and nationalistic sentiments were spreading among the German-speaking Austrian population—especially among the middle- and upper-class elements on which the government depended to staff the bureaucracy. Although Francis failed to respond to the nationalistic movement, he did not totally ignore his subjects' interests. He attempted to restore a measure of economic prosperity throughout the empire, which was suffering from inflation as a result of the expensive and protracted Napoleonic wars.

Superficially Francis' rule had seemed capable of containing the forces of revolution, nationalism, and liberal ideals of representative government. This apparent complacency was challenged, however, in the revolution-plagued year of 1848. In this year liberalism and nationalism collided; it was nationalism that survived the clash. A revolution in Sicily began a chain reaction of popular uprisings demanding political liberty all over Europe. In Italy, Austrian forces were expelled from Milan and Venice, and the peninsula seemed on the verge of unification.

By this time, the Austrian crown had passed to the imbecilic Ferdinand I, with social unrest in the em-

Above, members of the Civic Guard, formed at Vienna in April 1848 after the imperial army had been withdrawn from the city to deal with uprisings elsewhere. The guards, chiefly middle-class burghers (merchants or traders) and students, demanded the convocation of a constitutional national assembly. Right, Emperor Ferdinand I, who succeeded his father Francis I in 1835 and was forced to abdicate in favor of his eighteen-year-old nephew Francis Joseph in December 1848. An imbecile and epileptic, Ferdinand was unable to deal with the revolutionary situation of 1848.

148

Left, barricades on the Michaelerplatz, in Vienna, May 1848. Street demonstrations against Hapsburg rule broke out in the capital following news of the French Revolution, which deposed Louis Philippe. The city's middle classes drew up petitions demanding freedom of the press, trial by jury, civil rights, an end to religious discrimination, full emancipation for peasants, and a constitutional and representative government. The unrest soon spread to the lower classes, and the imperial court was forced to leave Vienna for Innsbruck.

In October of 1848, imperial troops bombarded the gates of Vienna (right). After a week-long siege against the revolutionaries, order was restored to the capital by two armies led by Josip Jelačić and Prince Alfred Windisch-Graetz of Styria. Soon afterward Prince Felix von Schwarzenberg became prime minister of Austria and Emperor Ferdinand I abdicated his throne.

pire intensified by a serious economic depression in the 1840s. In March of 1848 news reached Vienna that revolution had broken out in Paris, touching off street demonstrations against Metternich's "system" in Vienna and other cities. Metternich fled in disguise to England, and the Austrian people were promised a constitution.

The middle-class German Austrians, who assumed that they would be the dominant element in a new, liberalized empire, were quickly alarmed by working-class uprisings and by the demands of the Czechs and other Slavic nationalities for autonomy within a federalized Austrian Empire. The only people with whom the German liberals found they could coexist were the Magyars, or Hungarians, who, under the demogogic leadership of Louis Kossuth, were trying to dominate the non-Hungarian majority living in their country and deprive them of their rights.

The divisions among the opponents of the Hapsburg government, as well as the army's continued loyalty, enabled the Hapsburgs to survive the revolu-

Top, Charles Albert, king of the Italian region of Sardinia-Piedmont from 1831 to 1849, during the turbulent period of the political unification that was part of the Italian Risorgimento. Charles Albert saw himself as Italy's liberator; he declared war on Austria after the Milanese revolution of March 1848. Although at first he was very successful, he was defeated at Custoza and Milan in June and signed an armistice in August. Immediately above, barricades at Tosa Gate, in the rebellious city of Milan, March 1848. Right, Austrian troops attacking the ancient canal city of Venice, which also rebelled against Austrian rule in March 1848.

tions of 1848. To the applause of the German Austrians, the army bombarded the Czech capital of Prague into submission in June of 1848 and disbanded the Slav Congress that had been meeting there. After continued working-class demonstrations, the army also took control of Vienna in October 1848. Hapsburg forces meanwhile defeated the armies of the Italian states and restored the dynasty's supremacy in Italy. At the end of 1848, Emperor Ferdinand, under a government newly formed by Prime Minister Felix von Schwarzenberg, was prevailed upon to abdicate in favor of his eighteen-year-old nephew, Francis Joseph, primarily to allow concessions promised in Ferdinand's name to be repudiated by a new emperor.

The following spring Hapsburg troops, supported by Croat and Romanian nationalists, marched against Hungary, which had recently declared its independence. The Hungarians' resistance was initially successful, forcing the Hapsburgs to call in the Rus-

Above left, a scene from the battle of Goito, May 30, 1848. The Piedmontese forces led by Charles Albert, king of Sardinia-Piedmont, defeated the imperial army commanded by the eighty-two-year-old Austrian field marshal Joseph Radetzky. The Piedmontese, however, failed to follow up their advantage and were decisively defeated at Custoza in June. During 1848–1849, Italians were taken prisoner (above) in the Hapsburgs' campaigns to quell nationalistic revolutionary uprisings in Italy. Right, Austrian troops re-entering Milan in July 1848, following the battle of Custoza. Milan's five-day revolt in March had forced Field Marshal Radetzky to withdraw and fight a defensive war against a coalition of Italian forces gathered in northern Italy.

Above, the beautiful and romantic Elizabeth of Bavaria, whom Francis Joseph married in 1854. She was his first cousin, coming from a dynasty related to the Hapsburgs by many marriages. Their marriage soon became plagued with problems: Elizabeth hated the many constraints of court life in Vienna, resented her young husband's zeal for hard work, and heartily disliked her interfering, tyrannical mother-in-law, Archduchess Sophia. Elizabeth's longing for freedom was expressed in sad little poems and a passion for long, solitary rides. Francis Joseph remained very much in love with "Sisi," as he called her, despite her tantrums, depressions, and spells of coldness. Above right, the young emperor and his wife out on a carriage ride.

Right, a painting of Francis Joseph on horseback. The emperor ascended the throne in 1848—following his uncle Ferdinand's forced abdication—and was destined to occupy it for almost seventy years. During his reign he saw Prussia's rise to dominance in Germany, the unification of Italy, his empire's transformation into a dual Austro-Hungarian Empire, and the outbreak of a cataclysmic world war. Francis Joseph's subjects generally found him kind and polite, and eventually came to admire him.

Left, a chaotic moment of indecision at the battle of Solferino on June 24, 1859, during which both the imperial army, under Francis Joseph, and the Franco-Piedmontese forces, led by Napoleon III, lost control over their men. The defeated Austrians suffered so many casualties that Francis Joseph said: "Rather lose a province than undergo such a horrible experience again." Napoleon III and Francis Joseph (below, left and right, respectively) met at Villafranca after the battle to negotiate peace.

Following pages, the state funeral of Field Marshal Radetzky, who died in Milan in 1858, at the age of ninety-two. Born in Bohemia and educated at Maria Theresa's military academy in Vienna, Radetzky joined the imperial army in 1785. He emerged from virtual retirement to save the Austrian Empire from destruction in 1848–1849.

sian armies of Czar Nicholas I. Russian intervention turned the tide, and the Hungarians capitulated in August of 1849. "Hungary now lies at the feet of Your Majesty," Nicholas wrote to Francis Joseph. Schwarzenberg, however, did not relish the prospect of Austria becoming a Russian dependency and was moved to remark: "We shall astound the world with our ingratitude."

A decade of renewed absolutism followed the suppression of the Hungarian bid for independence. The constitution proposed during the revolution was thrust aside; Francis Joseph proclaimed himself absolute ruler of the monarchy, centralized the Ger-

man-speaking bureaucracy under his direct control, and restored rigid censorship. The only legacy of the revolution to survive was the abolition of the last vestiges of serfdom.

By refusing to back Russia during the Crimean War (1853–1856), Austria helped to ensure the czar's defeat by the British and French, thus deepening Russian bitterness toward the Hapsburgs and encouraging a Russian shift away from its former allies. In 1859 the Italian kingdom of Piedmont, backed by Napoleon III, successfully wrested from Austrian rule the province of Lombardy. Italian unification followed rapidly, and national disaffection

153

Maximilian in Mexico

Francis Joseph's younger brother, Maximilian, began his career in the navy. After quickly rising to a high level of command, he became, in 1857, viceroy of the Lombardo-Venetian kingdom. At the outbreak of Austria's war with Piedmont and France in 1859, Maximilian retired to private life, in which he amused himself by directing the building of a castle and by exploring Brazil's tropical forests in search of exotic botanical specimens. At the urging of Napoleon III, who needed help in furthering French interests in Central America, Maximilian agreed to accept the proffered crown of Mexico in 1863, despite Francis Joseph's opposition. Unfortunately, in response to a demand of the United States government, Napoleon III withdrew his troops from Mexico in 1864. Although Maximilian struggled to maintain his rule against heavy odds, he was overthrown and executed by Mexican troops in 1867.

Left, Mexican exiles under French patronage offering the imperial crown of Mexico to Maximilian at the Adriatic seaport of Trieste, in 1863. His ambitious wife, Princess Charlotte, daughter of Belgian king Leopold I, urged him to accept; her folly was later to drive her mad. Below left, a partial view of the castle of Miramare and its surrounding park, built by Maximilian near Trieste in the popular medieval style of the time.

Top left, Maximilian and Charlotte departing for Mexico, full of hopes and illusions. Top right, a Mexican celebration in honor of Benito Juárez, who had overthrown Emperor Maximilian. Above, three of Maximilian's soldiers. Maximilian was shot with two of his generals (below left) at Querétaro, even though many European governments and individuals, including French writer Victor Hugo and Italian patriot Giuseppe Garibaldi, had tried to save his life. Below, a detail depicting Maximilian's body arriving at Trieste prior to burial in the imperial vault at Vienna.

Tale of two powers

Although Austria and Prussia were at odds for most of the nineteenth century, they cooperated in 1864 in a joint invasion of Denmark and a successful conquest of Schleswig and Holstein. The ownership of these two duchies northwest of Prussia had long been contested, for although Holstein was held by the king of Denmark, it was a German-speaking province. In November 1863, Prussia and Austria took advantage of the death of the Danish king Frederick VII—who had left no heirs—by making the province part of the German Confederation. Prussian troops under Prince Friedrich Karl seized the strategically important Danish fortress of Dybbøl, and an Austrian naval squadron under Admiral Wilhelm von Tegetthoff broke a Danish blockade. In 1866, Prussia ousted Austria from the province and soon became the dominant power in northern Germany.

Top, the battle of Vis (Lissa) in the Gulf of Venice during the Italian-Austrian War of 1866. The Austrian admiral, Count Wilhelm von Tegetthoff, sank three Italian ironclads, killing one thousand Italians. Immediately above, the battle of Königgrätz (Sadowa) on July 3, 1866, in present-day Czechoslovakia. The Prussian army under General von Moltke inflicted a crushing defeat on the Austrians. The battle, which helped Prussia to become the dominant power in Germany, demonstrated the superiority of Prussian breechloading "needle guns" and open infantry formations over Austrian muzzleloaders and massed bayonet charges.

spread among both the Germans and the Hungarians. The following year Francis Joseph conceded a new constitution that, while establishing a central parliament to which all local estates might send delegates, favored the German-speaking element—to the outrage of the Slavs and Hungarians.

During the decade of the sixties, the Hapsburgs struggled in vain to retain their primacy in the German Confederation—established in 1815 after the Napoleonic wars—and to uphold the principle of administrative centralization in the empire. In 1863 Francis Joseph convened a meeting of all the princes belonging to the German Confederation in the hope of revising its structure and placing it under his authority, thereby assuming leadership of the German national cause. Unfortunately for Francis Joseph, the Prussian king William I also wanted to dominate the Confederation—as well as destroy Hapsburg power in Germany.

The Hapsburgs suffered their first major German defeat between 1863 and 1866, when Prussia, led by the exceptionally able prime minister Otto von Bismarck, assumed the leadership of the German cause. War broke out between the two rivals in 1866, and Austria met with a crushing defeat, partly because of unrest among the Hungarians and a diversionary attack by the Italians (who annexed Venetia after the

Left, a popular sketch of the heroes of the battle of Vis, with Admiral Tegetthoff located at the top center. Most of the admiral's sailors were Venetians or Dalmatians—Italians like their adversaries—but their loyalty was to the Hapsburgs. The Austrians' land victory at Custoza in June 1866 and their sea victory off the island of Vis in July helped to offset their humiliating defeat at Königgrätz.

Above, a scene depicting Austrian hussars, or horsemen of the light cavalry, attacking the Prussian infantry at the battle of Königgrätz, painted by A. von Benso. The hussars, who originated in fifteenth-century Hungary, typically wore brilliantly colored uniforms consisting of a busby, or tall, cylindrical cloth hat; a heavily braided jacket; and a capelike dolman worn over the left shoulder.

The imperial army

After the Congress of Vienna in 1815, Francis I began to economize on the imperial forces. Between 1815 and 1850 there were only about two hundred thousand men in the army, less than half of the preferred norm during times of peace. Most of these troops were undesirables rejected by the local authorities. A lack of modern equipment also hindered the army's effectiveness. The battle of Königgrätz in 1866, in which the Austrians were soundly defeated by the well-organized and up-to-date Prussians, highlighted the need for reform. In an effort to improve the situation, Francis Joseph appointed his brother, Archduke Albrecht, inspector general of the army and instructed him to institute changes. The archduke quickly re-equipped the imperial infantry with breechloading rifles and the artillery with the latest guns. He also introduced three years' compulsory service for all able-bodied men in the monarchy and promoted passage of a law that required both Austria and Hungary to decide, every ten years, on the number of recruits they would provide in the next decade. By these means the strength of the imperial units and reserves quickly rose (at least on paper) to eight hundred thousand. Although equipment and military tactics were based primarily on Prussian ideas developed by General von Moltke, the imperial army retained its own individuality and unique multinational character up until the final days of the Hapsburg Empire.

On May 9, 1864, a gala dinner (facing page, center) for officers of the imperial army was held at Schönbrunn Palace, in the presence of the emperor. Facing page, bottom left, a drummer and a lance-corporal of the Austro-Hungarian army. The language of command in the joint army was German, although the Hungarians felt this detracted from their position of equal status. Facing page, bottom right, the Imperial Guards on parade. The purpose of this elite corps, mostly drawn from the nobility, was to protect the imperial family.

Right, a hurdle race in 1856 among members of the Austrian army at Padua, in northeastern Italy. Below, the Hoch- und Deutschmeister Regiment, dating back to a German order of the 1530s, on parade. Each regiment in the army carefully cultivated its own traditions. Colonel Count Pejacevic (bottom left) was commander of the Ninth Hussar Regiment during the German-Danish War of 1864. The hussars, specializing in reconnaissance and raiding, were first recruited by the fifteenth-century Hungarian king Matthias Corvinus to fight the Turks.

Below right, three soldiers in uniforms typically worn by members of the Austro-Hungarian army in the second half of the nineteenth century.

war, thus removing Austria's last stronghold in the Italian peninsula). Austria was excluded from a drastically revised German Confederation imposed by Prussian arms. In 1871 William I was proclaimed German emperor. Nationalism had proved to be too potent and too divisive: The Hapsburg Empire now would have to come to terms with the demands of this movement or face the chilling prospect of eventual collapse.

In the aftermath of the Hapsburgs' defeat in Germany and Italy, Francis Joseph was forced to settle with Hungary's moderate constitutional leaders, Ferencz Déak and Count Gyula Andrássy. The Compromise of 1867 established Hungary as a kingdom with its own internal autonomy and transformed the Austrian Empire into the Austro-Hungarian Empire, known as the "dual monarchy." Within the revived kingdom of Hungary, the Magyars assumed uncontested supremacy and used their influence to prevent Francis Joseph from making similar concessions to the Czechs of Bohemia. In Galicia the Polish upper class was allowed domination over the Ukrainian element, and the province remained loyal to the Hapsburgs until 1918. During the early 1870s Austria-Hungary concluded an alliance with Germany, and despite major differences, the two empires remained allies until both were swept away by defeat in World War One.

The Compromise of 1867 thus only partly alleviated the Hapsburgs' difficulties in dealing with the rival nationalisms of the people over whom they ruled. The Hungarians, Germans, and Poles had been satisfied, but only at the expense of increased alienation among the Czechs, Slovaks, Croats, Serbs, Romanians, and Ukrainians. In this respect Francis Joseph's problems were ultimately insoluable, for had he come to terms with the latter nationalities, he would have faced the protracted resistance of the first three.

The empire survived its last half-century, from 1867 to 1918, largely by inertia. Rival nationalisms tended to cancel each other out; social antagonisms were mitigated by the economic prosperity that had come to the Danubian basin. Government by bureaucratic decree was not only possible but almost inevitable. Until World War One most of the disaffected nationalities aimed less at independence than at autonomy and the domination of their neighbors. It was generally recognized that, for all its faults, the Hapsburg monarchy gave economic unity to the Danubian basin; both the Social Democratic Party and the Austro-Hungarian capitalists realized the desirability of maintaining the empire as an economic entity. As he aged and suffered many personal tribu-

Above, the Parliament Building in Budapest, viewed from across the Danube. Immediately below, Viennese onlookers viewing a military parade. Bottom, a 1904 gathering around Dr. Karl Lueger, the civic-minded mayor of Vienna, in the city's principal park, the Prater.

Far right, the launching of the great battleship Viribus Unitis, *in 1911. Right, the German emperor William II (fifth from right) congratulating Francis Joseph on the fiftieth year of his reign as emperor of Austria.*

Francis Joseph

Right, the archduke Francis Ferdinand's bloodstained tunic after his assassination at Sarajevo in June of 1914. Below left, a portrait of Francis Ferdinand in military uniform. The heir to the Austro-Hungarian throne was not close to his uncle, Francis Joseph.

During his long reign (1848–1916), Francis Joseph not only endured severe military and diplomatic upsets, but also suffered several family tragedies. His brother Maximilian, disregarding his advice on the dangers of accepting the Mexican crown, was overthrown and shot to death in 1867. In 1889 Francis Joseph experienced another misfortune—the mysterious and highly embarrassing suicide of his only son and heir, Rudolf. The following decade saw the assassination of his beloved wife Elizabeth by a crazed Italian anarchist. Finally, his nephew Francis Ferdinand, heir to the throne, was murdered by Bosnian-Serbian nationalists at Sarajevo, Bosnia, in 1914. Although Francis Joseph was not overly saddened by Francis Ferdinand's death (he disapproved of his nephew's strong character and pro-Slav politics), he did feel some remorse when his declaration of war against Serbia triggered a world war.

Below center, a Bosnian student, Gavrilo Princip, shooting the archduke Francis Ferdinand and his wife Countess Sophie Chotek, as they drive through the streets of Sarajevo. The murder provided an excuse for Austria-Hungary to attack Serbia, a hotbed of anti-Hapsburg nationalism.

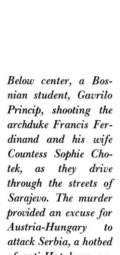

Crowds thronged the banks of the Neretva River (left) to view the ship bearing the coffins of Francis Ferdinand and his wife to sea. The bodies then were placed on board the Viribus Unitis, sailed to the city of Trieste, and carried by train to Vienna, where a state funeral was held.

Right, Rudolf, Francis Joseph's only son and heir. Although intelligent and a brilliant marksman, Rudolf was prone to morbid depressions. In January 1889 he unexpectedly committed suicide with his seventeen-year-old mistress, Baroness Maria Vetsera, in the Hapsburg hunting lodge of Mayerling (below), near Vienna.

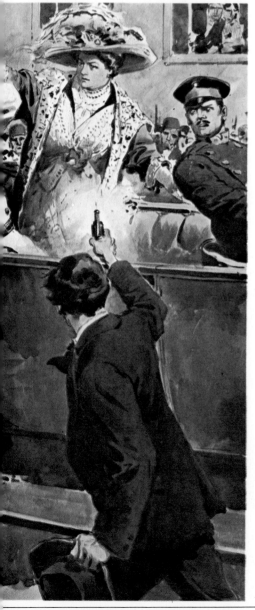

lations, Francis Joseph came to be thought of as a noble symbol of order and stability—a monarch who transcended national conflicts.

Prestige was also awarded to Vienna during the last half-century of the Austro-Hungarian Empire, when the capital city emerged as one of prewar Europe's great cultural and intellectual centers. During this period, the city hosted composers Johann Strauss, Johannes Brahms, and Gustav Mahler; playwrights Hugo von Hofmannsthal and Arthur Schnitzler; and Sigmund Freud, the father of psychoanalysis. The slums of Vienna also harbored an unknown vagrant named Adolf Hitler.

Although peace probably would have allowed the Hapsburg Empire to survive indefinitely in some form, it could not survive defeat in a twentieth-century war. Austria-Hungary's government bore a large responsibility for unleashing World War One by directing an attack on Serbia in 1914 in an effort to crush the nationalist movement that had organized the assassination of Archduke Francis Ferdinand, heir to the Hapsburg throne.

Many of the Slavic and Romanian soldiers in the Hapsburg armies felt less and less loyalty to the empire's cause as the war dragged on. The Austro-Hungarian forces, defeated in almost every major encounter, had to be rescued by the Germans. Inefficiency

and corruption aggravated the usual wartime shortages of food, fuel, and consumer goods, and on the home front war-weariness soon became overpowering. As one German journalist appropriately described it: "In Berlin the situation is serious but not desperate; in Vienna it is desperate but not serious." Francis Joseph's death in 1916—ending one of the longest reigns in recorded history—removed a familiar symbol of imperial unity.

His young successor Charles I's bungling efforts to extricate the empire from the war and to settle national antagonisms only served to encourage the German Empire to tighten control over the Hapsburg state and to speed up the nationalities' defection from the Hapsburg cause. By 1916 émigré spokesmen for the nationalities, such as the Czech leader T. G. Masaryk, had won the support of the Western Allies, and it became increasingly evident that an Allied victory would soon bring about the destruction of the Hapsburg Empire in the name of "national self-determination."

The defeat of the German and Austro-Hungarian armies in 1918 made the final catastrophe inevitable. In the fall of 1918 one national group after another declared its independence, and the German Austrians made a futile attempt to join the German Reich (Empire). The partition of the Austro-Hungarian

Above, a patrol on the Kras, a mountain plateau on the Italian-Yugoslavian border, during World War One. In the two battles that were fought here in May of 1916 and 1917, the Italians vanquished the Austrians. Right, the Jäger Regiment, from Tyrol. The Austro-Hungarian army, while not prepared for a protracted European war fought on several fronts, managed to continue in the field for four years, despite numerous defeats.

Above, the emperor's study in the Hofburg, in which Charles I renounced all participation in affairs of state after the collapse of the Austro-Hungarian forces in November 1918. By this act Charles formally dissolved the Hapsburg monarchy.

Above, Francis Joseph in the last years of his sixty-eight-year reign. He died in 1916 while World War One was in full force and did not live to see the complete disintegration of the centuries-old Hapsburg Empire, which he had done his utmost to uphold.

The last Hapsburg emperor, young Charles I (right), succeeded Francis Joseph in 1916. Although he was intelligent and capable of making sound judgments, Charles was slow to act. His promise of autonomy to the various nationalities in the dual monarchy of Austria-Hungary came in August 1918—too late to prevent the subsequent dissolution of the empire into the successor states of Czechoslovakia, Poland, Romania, Yugoslavia, Hungary, and Austria. He abdicated the throne in 1918 and was formally deposed by the Austrian Parliament in April of 1919. After two unsuccessful attempts to regain the crown of Hungary, Charles retired to the island of Madeira, where he died in 1922.

Empire into the "successor states" of Czechoslovakia, Yugoslavia, Romania, and Poland and the survival of the truncated, economically crippled states of Austria and Hungary were sanctioned by the postwar treaties of St. Germain and Trianon.

Although the Hapsburg Empire is gone, the spirit of multinational federalism has not disappeared entirely. Nor is the Hapsburg dynasty extinct. It seems peculiarly appropriate that the first parliament elected by the nine nations of the European Economic Community in 1979 included the multilingual jurist Doctor Otto von Hapsburg—the eldest son of the last Hapsburg emperor, Charles I.

Photography Credits

Index